> *I was a kid who went to Italy and got involved in the war there.*
>
> —Hemingway's response to the question "What got you started writing A Farewell to Arms?"

Contents

Foreword 8

Introduction 10

Ernest Hemingway: A Biographical Sketch 12

Characters and Plot 30

Chapter 1: Background to *A Farewell to Arms*

1. **The Writing of the Novel** *by Jeffrey Meyers* 38
   A Farewell to Arms is not intended to be a nonfictional account of Hemingway's experiences in Italy during World War I. Though many of the events in the novel are drawn from real life, Hemingway believed in "inventing from knowledge," which entails altering actual events to create art through fiction.

2. **The Euphemistic Language of World War I** *by Paul Fussell* 44
   Before World War I, the language used to describe warfare was highly euphemistic, specifically designed to make war seem glorious and to hide its horrors, prompting impressionable young men to enlist eagerly. After the war, such innocence was impossible.

Chapter 2: Characters in *A Farewell to Arms*

1. **The Role of Catherine Barkley** *by Peter L. Hays* 49
   Catherine Barkley is much more than a passive female who is conveniently placed in the novel to serve as the object of Frederic's affections. Her limitations are those of any woman caught up in the horror of warfare, but her strengths far outweigh her weaknesses.

2. **Frederic Henry: A Selfish Lover** *by Scott Donaldson* 56
   Frederic and Catherine are not perfect lovers. Catherine's desire to lose herself to Frederic as a result of a previous failed relationship is excessive, while Frederic himself is far too selfish to form a bond with anyone.

3. Excerpt from *A Reader's Guide to Ernest Hemingway:* **A Farewell to Arms**
   by *Arthur Waldhorn*   68
   Frederic Henry must make his way in the world between two opposing role models, Rinaldi and the priest. Rinaldi, Frederic's roommate, is a cynical and pleasure-seeking army surgeon. Conversely, the priest counsels Frederic to discover the spiritual world and forsake the profane lifestyle of the common soldier.

4. **Frederic's and Catherine's Role Reversal**
   by *Michael S. Reynolds*   72
   Early in the novel, Frederic, the wounded war hero, has the more obvious claim to heroism. But as the novel progresses, Hemingway diminishes Frederic in a series of scenes that fracture and negate his identity and propel Catherine Barkley into the role of the novel's heroine.

Chapter 3: Major Themes

1. **Frederic Henry's Heroic Rejection of Clichés**
   by *Blanche Gelfant*   78
   A major theme of *A Farewell to Arms* is the rejection of the old, euphemistic clichés of warfare: words such as "sacred," "glorious," "sacrifice," and "in vain." But when faced with Catherine's death, Frederic briefly falls back on similar clichés. Ultimately, he must face this dire event without the crutch of clichéd language.

2. **Frederic Henry's Disillusionment with War**
   by *Jackson J. Benson*   83
   Frederic Henry, a purposeless young man, has joined the war effort for no real reason. After being wounded, he begins to see the reality of war, and the manner in which warfare strips individuals of their identity. This is a game Frederic no longer wishes to play, so he runs off with Catherine Barkley.

3. **Time and Mortality in *A Farewell to Arms***
   by *D. Quentin Miller*   95
   Throughout *a Farewell to Arms*, Hemingway manipulates the way his protagonist refers to time. Because a soldier knows that any moment may be his last, for much of the novel Frederic attempts to avoid clock time and offers the reader few time references. When confronted with especially deadly situations, however, Frederic is highly aware of the time.

4. **Enduring Values in the Lost Generation**
   by *Joseph Warren Beach*   100
   The 1920s was an era famous for a lack of values that many see as a response to the horrors of World War I. Despite the tendency to live solely for pleasure, Frederic and

Catherine support each other with love and courage. Their virtues are impressive in a world filled with turmoil and destruction.

5. **The General Versus the Specific in**
   A Farewell to Arms **by Floyd C. Watkins**   106
   Hemingway everywhere pits the vague abstractions of war against the individual needs of men. This juxtaposition is reflected in his style as well as in his theme. Ultimately Frederic Henry leaves the group for self-preservation.

Chapter 4: The Novelist's Technique

1. **The Original Opening of** *A Farewell to Arms*
   by Bernard Oldsey   116
   The original manuscript of the novel begins when a wounded Frederic Henry arrives at the hospital in Milan, where he meets Catherine Barkley. Hemingway later decided not to start the story in the middle, as he commonly did in other works, but to use a more straightforward, chronological narration.

2. **Two Plots in** *A Farewell to Arms*
   by Philip Young   127
   Two connected plots, that of the war and that of Frederic's love affair with Catherine, give *A Farewell to Arms* its structure. The novel has a pervading sense of doom, symbolized by rain, which hangs over the novel until the two plots merge with the death of Catherine Barkley.

3. **The Symbolic Structure of** *A Farewell to Arms*
   by Carlos Baker   133
   From the opening scene of the book, the mountains and the plain are used as contrasting motifs that give *A Farewell to Arms* its symbolic structure. The plain is associated with the war, suffering, and disease, while the mountains, preferred by the priest as a place of spirituality, offer an escape from the degradation of war.

4. **Hemingway's Use of Details**
   by Sheldon Norman Grebstein   139
   Hemingway was a master of specific detail used to characterize and to suggest larger themes. In two passages in *A Farewell to Arms*, he invests powerful emotions in these details.

5. **Hemingway's Baby Talk**
   by Dwight Macdonald   142
   Writing in a style that parodies Hemingway's simple word choice and sentence structure, the author states the case against *A Farewell to Arms* and Hemingway's novels in general. Hemingway was a talented writer of short stories, but

THE GREENHAVEN PRESS
Literary Companion
TO AMERICAN LITERATURE

READINGS ON

A FAREWELL TO ARMS

Gary Wiener, *Book Editor*

David L. Bender, *Publisher*
Bruno Leone, *Executive Editor*
Bonnie Szumski, *Series Editor*

Greenhaven Press, Inc., San Diego, CA

Every effort has been made to trace the owners of copyrighted material. The articles in this volume may have been edited for content, length, and/or reading level. The titles have been changed to enhance the editorial purpose. Those interested in locating the original source will find the complete citation on the first page of each article.

Library of Congress Cataloging-in-Publication Data

Readings on A farewell to arms / Gary Wiener, book editor.
    p.   cm. — (Greenhaven Press literary companion to American literature)
    Includes bibliographical references and index.
    ISBN 0-7377-0232-X (pbk. : alk. paper). — ISBN 0-7377-0233-8 (lib. : alk. paper)
    1. Hemingway, Ernest, 1899–1961. Farewell to arms. 2. World War, 1914–1918—Literature and the war. I. Wiener, Gary. II. Title: Farewell to arms. III. Series.
PS3515.E37F3577   2000
813'.52—dc21   99-25705
                                                              CIP

Cover photo: Corbis

   No part of this book may be reproduced or used in any form or by any means, electrical, mechanical, or otherwise, including, but not limited to, photocopy, recording, or any information storage and retrieval system, without prior written permission from the publisher.

Copyright © 2000 by Greenhaven Press, Inc.
PO Box 289009
San Diego, CA 92198-9009
Printed in the U.S.A.

his style becomes tedious when he tries to sustain it over the course of a longer work.

6. A Simple Tale *by Clifton Fadiman* — 147
At a time when most celebrated novels were complex and difficult to understand, Ernest Hemingway gave his readers a simple love story. The novel draws its power from this simplicity, and from the intensity of feeling that Hemingway creates.

Chronology	150
For Further Research	153
Index	155

Foreword

> *"'Tis the good reader that
> makes the good book."*
>
> Ralph Waldo Emerson

The story's bare facts are simple: The captain, an old and scarred seafarer, walks with a peg leg made of whale ivory. He relentlessly drives his crew to hunt the world's oceans for the great white whale that crippled him. After a long search, the ship encounters the whale and a fierce battle ensues. Finally the captain drives his harpoon into the whale, but the harpoon line catches the captain about the neck and drags him to his death.

A simple story, a straightforward plot—yet, since the 1851 publication of Herman Melville's *Moby-Dick*, readers and critics have found many meanings in the struggle between Captain Ahab and the whale. To some, the novel is a cautionary tale that depicts how Ahab's obsession with revenge leads to his insanity and death. Others believe that the whale represents the unknowable secrets of the universe and that Ahab is a tragic hero who dares to challenge fate by attempting to discover this knowledge. Perhaps Melville intended Ahab as a criticism of Americans' tendency to become involved in well-intentioned but irrational causes. Or did Melville model Ahab after himself, letting his fictional character express his anger at what he perceived as a cruel and distant god?

Although literary critics disagree over the meaning of *Moby-Dick*, readers do not need to choose one particular interpretation in order to gain an understanding of Melville's novel. Instead, by examining various analyses, they can gain numerous insights into the issues that lie under the surface of the basic plot. Studying the writings of literary critics can also aid readers in making their own assessments of *Moby-Dick* and other literary works and in developing analytical thinking skills.

The Greenhaven Literary Companion Series was created with these goals in mind. Designed for young adults, this unique anthology series provides an engaging and comprehensive introduction to literary analysis and criticism. The essays included in the Literary Companion Series are chosen for their accessibility to a young adult audience and are expertly edited in consideration of both the reading and comprehension levels of this audience. In addition, each essay is introduced by a concise summation that presents the contributing writer's main themes and insights. Every anthology in the Literary Companion Series contains a varied selection of critical essays that cover a wide time span and express diverse views. Wherever possible, primary sources are represented through excerpts from authors' notebooks, letters, and journals and through contemporary criticism.

Each title in the Literary Companion Series pays careful consideration to the historical context of the particular author or literary work. In-depth biographies and detailed chronologies reveal important aspects of authors' lives and emphasize the historical events and social milieu that influenced their writings. To facilitate further research, every anthology includes primary and secondary source bibliographies of articles and/or books selected for their suitability for young adults. These engaging features make the Greenhaven Literary Companion series ideal for introducing students to literary analysis in the classroom or as a library resource for young adults researching the world's great authors and literature.

Exceptional in its focus on young adults, the Greenhaven Literary Companion Series strives to present literary criticism in a compelling and accessible format. Every title in the series is intended to spark readers' interest in leading American and world authors, to help them broaden their understanding of literature, and to encourage them to formulate their own analyses of the literary works that they read. It is the editors' hope that young adult readers will find these anthologies to be true companions in their study of literature.

Introduction

Not until the 1950s did one of the most famous living writers in the world, Ernest Hemingway, begin to receive the awards from the literary establishment that were clearly his due. In 1953 and 1954, Hemingway collected both the Pulitzer Prize for fiction and the Nobel Prize in literature. The immediate incentive for these awards was the recent publication of his novella *The Old Man and the Sea*, but while that work is justly considered a classic in its own right, there is no doubt that Hemingway's awards, especially the Nobel, were the fruits of a lifetime of writing. Most readers of Hemingway would agree that he produced his finest writing in his early years, particularly between 1925 and 1940, when he wrote *The Sun Also Rises*, *A Farewell to Arms*, and *For Whom the Bell Tolls*, along with numerous brilliant short stories.

A Farewell to Arms, Hemingway's second novel, fictionalizes two major events in his life: his July 8, 1918, wounding at the Italian front in World War I and his subsequent affair with an American army nurse named Agnes von Kurowsky. Though some readers disparage the novel's characters, particularly the women, and others find fault with the minimalistic dialogue that was a Hemingway trademark, most finish *A Farewell to Arms* with the sense that it is a work of genius. Hemingway's stylistic innovation and dramatic honesty place him among the greatest writers of his time.

The poet Walt Whitman once said with regard to the American Civil War, "The real war will never get in the books." Until writers such as e.e. cummings, Wilfred Owen, Siegfried Sassoon, and Ernest Hemingway went to World War I, Whitman was very nearly correct. It was Hemingway's generation that first refused to sugarcoat the horrors of war with euphemistic phrases designed to inspire impressionable youths to battle. Commenting that the traditional vocabulary felt uncomfortable once one had actually seen the war, Hemingway wrote in *A Farewell to Arms* what are arguably his most famous lines. After a fellow soldier says, "We won't talk about losing. . . . What has been done this summer cannot have been done in vain," Hemingway's protagonist, Frederic Henry, responds:

> I was always embarrassed by the words sacred, glorious, and sacrifice and the expression in vain. We had heard them, sometimes standing in the rain almost out of earshot, so that only the shouted words came through, and had read them, on proclamations that were slapped up by billposters over other proclamations, now for a long time, and I had seen nothing sacred, and things that were glorious had no glory and the sacrifices were like the stockyards at Chicago if nothing was done with the meat except to bury it. There were many words that you could not stand to hear and finally only the names of places had dignity. Certain numbers were the same way and certain dates and these with the names of the places were all you could say and have them mean anything. Abstract words such as glory, honor, courage or hallow were obscene beside the concrete names of villages, the numbers of roads, the names of rivers, the numbers of regiments and the dates.

In *A Farewell to Arms*, Ernest Hemingway told the truth. After Frederic is wounded in the trenches, the Italian army wants to decorate him for valor. "Did you do any heroic act?" his friend and roommate, the army surgeon Rinaldi, asks. "No," Frederic responds with typical candor, "I was blown up while we were eating cheese."

Ironically, Hemingway's honest portrayal of the love affair of Frederic and Catherine might have cost *A Farewell to Arms* early admission into the ranks of award-winning novels. As writer W.J. Stuckey suggests, in 1929 "a novel that presented, for the reader's approval, a physical love affair outside of marriage—no matter how many justifications were offered—was not likely to win the favorable notice of men who gave prizes to novels that condemned such relationships." In a year that saw publication not only of Hemingway's novel but of William Faulkner's masterpiece, *The Sound and the Fury*, the Pulitzer judges found Oliver La Farge's now-forgotten novel, *Laughing Boy*, more to their liking. Such is the nature of literary history, but the truest books live on. Their real reward is that each new generation of readers can learn and live from the lessons of the past.

ERNEST HEMINGWAY: A BIOGRAPHICAL SKETCH

That Ernest Hemingway's life was exhilarating, action-packed, and even, perhaps, heroic is no exaggeration. If excitement did not come to Hemingway, the writer sought it out. Trained as a journalist, he learned early on to find the captivating story and to translate the action to the reader via his hard, clean, spare prose style. Despite a host of fine novels and brilliant short stories, however, Hemingway's most studied story may be that of his own life. Throughout his career he worked hard to create a persona, who, real or imagined, was every bit as big, boisterous, and hard-living as protagonists Frederic Henry (*A Farewell to Arms*), Jacob Barnes (*The Sun Also Rises*), and Robert Jordan (*For Whom the Bell Tolls*). While biographers of Hemingway such as Kenneth Lynn and James R. Mellow have sought to separate the legend from the life, for many years the life of Ernest Miller Hemingway was as engrossing a fiction as any of his great novels. His story included working as a reporter, boxing as an amateur, driving an ambulance during World War I, covering World War II and the Spanish Civil War as a correspondent, hunting big game in Africa, and deep-sea fishing in the Caribbean. He married four times and attracted numerous celebrity friends. He lived in Chicago, Paris, Key West, Cuba, and Idaho and traveled extensively. In the end, in imitation of his doctor father, he took his own life in a shockingly dramatic manner. No matter how assertively later biographers debunk certain episodes, it is all the stuff of legend, all pure Hemingway.

EARLY LIFE

Ernest Miller Hemingway was born in Oak Park, Illinois, a wealthy suburb of Chicago, in 1899. His mother, Grace Hall, had trained for a musical career, but a childhood bout with scarlet fever left her hypersensitive to light. Her debut at New

York City's Madison Square Garden was a miserable failure when she could not perform under the bright stage lights. Soon after returning to her home in Oak Park, Grace met and married Clarence Edmonds Hemingway, known to his friends as Ed. Clarence Hemingway, a physician, was a general practitioner who had treated Grace's mother during her final illness. The young couple lived in Grace's father's large house in Oak Park, across the street from Clarence Hemingway's parents. Grace began a second career as a music teacher, from which she earned a good living. In January 1898, the couple's first child, Marcelline, was born, and Ernest followed eighteen months later. The eccentric Grace Hemingway treated the children as twins, even dressing Ernest in girl's clothing. Grace went so far as to hold Marcelline back from school until September 1906, when Ernest was also ready to enroll. Since Marcelline was a year and a half older than her brother, she was both physically and emotionally more advanced than Ernest, and his frustration over this situation led to sibling rivalry.

The Hemingway family would eventually include five daughters and two sons. As the recipient of a privileged upper middle-class upbringing, Ernest had a fairly happy childhood. Grace was serious about her children's cultural education, taking them to the opera, the symphony, and the theater in Chicago. They also visited the Chicago Art Museum, which housed some of the world's great paintings. As director of the children's choir at the Third Congregational Church in Oak Park, Grace endeavored to include Ernest in the group. But after a few months, his voice abruptly changed, and the experiment ended promptly. Instead, young Ernest took up the cello, which he practiced, at his mother's insistence, an hour a day. But he displayed little aptitude for the instrument.

Hemingway relished his summers at the family cottage, called Windemere, on Walloon Lake in northern Michigan. Here Ernest learned early to fish and hunt, passions that would remain with him throughout his life. He enjoyed outdoor trips with his father, who taught him survival skills such as building a fire, cooking outdoors, and constructing a shelter. Nevertheless, Hemingway was often embarrassed by his father, whom he considered something of a weakling and a coward. Grace was the dominant figure in the family and Dr. Hemingway rarely won a dispute with her. Neighbors believed he was henpecked. Hemingway's lifelong fascination with courage, his philosophy of testing oneself and meeting adversity with "grace under pressure," was in part a response to his father's perceived weakness.

Though his parents foresaw a medical career for the boy, early on he began to show a talent with words. In 1911 he drew praise from his grammar school teacher for a story, "My First Sea Voyage," that recounted not his but his uncle's childhood experience. In adopting another persona, Ernest already began to display a knack for the creation of character.

Hemingway's high school career was relatively uneventful. He was a hard worker who maintained good grades. He displayed a passion for football, but until he sprouted several inches during his junior year, he was small for his age. Hemingway began boxing in his home with his friends, and, as he grew, often pummeled other boys. In later years he would claim that professionals had taught him to box, but the reality was that Hemingway was largely a self-taught pugilist.

Another somewhat incongruous passion that fascinated Hemingway was journalism. Hemingway contributed numerous articles to the school's weekly newspaper, the *Trapeze*. His interest in writing blossomed, and he published a boxing story about a manager who unsuccessfully tried to fix a fight in the school literary magazine. He also wrote a story based on his experiences with Native Americans he had known while at his summer home. By the time he graduated, the boy who had been among the smallest in his class stood nearly six feet tall and had filled out considerably. All of the elements of the "tough guy" writer were already in place as Hemingway entered the wider world.

KANSAS CITY

Hemingway's parents urged him to attend college, but he refused. Instead, he landed his first job as a reporter for the *Kansas City Star* through the influence of his uncle, Tyler Hemingway, who owned a business in Kansas City. He worked under assistant city editor C.G. "Pete" Wellington, who sent him on assignments covering crime scenes and accidents. Hemingway correctly believed that working as a reporter would help sharpen his writing style. Wellington taught his reporters to write with stylistic discipline, using short sentences, few adjectives, and no slang. Hemingway would later remark that "those were the best rules I ever learned for the business of writing." Hemingway's half-year stint in Kansas City was notable in two other ways: His beat reporting allowed him to gather material for several short stories, and he met Ted Brumback, a fellow *Star* reporter who had served as an ambulance driver for the Red Cross in France during the summer of 1917 and was eager to return. With World War I still raging in Europe, Brumback and Hemingway agreed to apply to the Red Cross as ambulance drivers.

ITALY

In April 1918 Hemingway and Brumback left Kansas City. They went fishing in Michigan and visited briefly with the Hemingways in Chicago before heading to New York. Despite his poor eyesight, Hemingway passed the Red Cross physical. On May 22, 1918, he and Brumback were shipped to Europe. Of his tour of duty during World War I, Hemingway would later say, "I was an awful dope when I went to the . . . war. I can remember just thinking that we were the home team and the Austrians were the visiting team." Hemingway and Brumback had hoped to serve in France, but they were instead sent to Schio, in Italy, where the work was so easy that the volunteers took to calling their quarters the Schio Country Club. But Hemingway found his new job dull, with long idle periods between ambulance runs. Passing much of his time playing baseball and swimming, he complained, "I'm fed up. There's nothing up here but scenery and too damn much of that." Boredom aside, Hemingway was very sociable, and met many new friends. One prominent new acquaintance was John Dos Passos, a Harvard University graduate who, like Brumback, had driven an ambulance in France before coming to Italy. Dos Passos was also an aspiring writer. (His trilogy, *U.S.A.*, would be considered a major American work of fiction.)

Hemingway longed to be closer to the action, so, at the first chance, he signed up for duty near the Italian front at Fossalta, where the Italians and Austrians were entrenched. Here, he volunteered at a Red Cross canteen, which functioned as a soldiers' club. Every day he would ride his bicycle to the front lines to distribute candy, cigarettes, and postcards to the Italian soldiers. On the evening of July 8, 1918, a mortar exploded in the trench where Hemingway was distributing chocolate, killing the man closest to the blast and wounding Hemingway and other nearby soldiers. In great pain, Hemingway lifted one wounded man and carried him behind the lines. As he was doing so, a bullet struck his knee. How he covered the remaining one hundred yards to the command post, he could never remember. Or so goes the version that Hemingway told to friends and journalists. Contemporary biographers such as Kenneth Lynn and James R. Mellow believe his report lacks credibility. How indeed could the severely wounded Hemingway have lifted a fellow fallen soldier and carried him to safety? Both Lynn and Mellow have come to believe a later Hemingway account, in which he admitted that the version of his wounding depicted in *A Farewell to Arms* comes closest to the truth. When asked about his possible heroic acts, Frederic Henry replies, "I didn't carry anybody. I couldn't move."

Hemingway was put on a stretcher, but, ironically, no ambulances were immediately available, and he lay with other casualties. As biographer Carlos Baker tells it, "His tunic and breeches were so thickly soaked with Italian blood [from the men wounded in the trench] that they [the doctors] thought at first he had been shot through the chest." Doctors would later remove twenty-eight fragments of shrapnel from his feet and legs, but hundreds of others were embedded too deeply to be safely removed.

Some biographers believe that Hemingway's wounding at the Italian front was the central event of his life. He took great pride in his 227 separate wounds, was commended by the Italian army, and modeled the key scene in *A Farewell to Arms* on this experience. Back home, newspaper accounts touted the bravery of the first American wounded in Italy. "It's great to be the mother of a hero," wrote Grace Hemingway.

Hemingway's own account of his wounding is perhaps as great a fiction as any he ever wrote. He downplayed any pain or suffering from his injuries:

> The wounds from the trench mortar didn't hurt a bit, and the machine gun bullet just felt like a smack on the leg by an icy snow ball. I got up and got my wounded to the dug-out.
>
> It gives you an awfully satisfactory feeling to be wounded; it's getting beaten up in a good cause. There are no heroes in this war. We all offer our bodies and only a few are chosen. They are the lucky ones. I am proud and happy that mine was chosen, but it shouldn't give me any extra credit.

Hemingway was taken to the American Red Cross hospital in Milan, Italy, where he underwent an operation to remove bullets from his kneecap and foot. He had the best of care. The hospital, established in a mansion, had eighteen nurses and only four patients. His surgeon, Captain Sammerelli, was highly skilled. Even so, as biographer Jeffrey Meyers writes, "The main attraction—and most effective therapy—at the hospital was a lovely American nurse, Agnes von Kurowsky, with whom Hemingway quickly and inevitably fell in love." All of the patients in the hospital admired the tall, slender brunette. Though dating soldiers was forbidden by Red Cross rules, and Agnes was not by nature a rule breaker, she did accept an invitation from an Italian captain, Enrico Serena, who was a regular visitor to the hospital. Serena befriended Hemingway, whom he called "Baby." He would become the model for the affable, cynical Captain Rinaldi in *A Farewell to Arms*.

Hemingway seemed to enjoy his recuperation. For a time there was mention of amputation of his badly wounded legs, but he instead insisted on the removal of every shard of embedded fragment "no matter how long it took or how great the pain." Hemingway even extracted some of the smaller fragments himself with a penknife, dulling the pain with a bottle of cognac that he kept hidden from the hospital staff. Infinitely more enjoyable were numerous visits from administrators, soldiers, and admirers who treated him like a king. Serena would often bring gifts. "You know how he was," Agnes von Kurowsky would later say. "Men loved him. You know what I mean."

Though Agnes was twenty-six years old, seven years Hemingway's senior, she began to return his affections. They spent a great deal of time together as Hemingway recovered his strength, aided by crutches and later a cane. But their affair never progressed beyond kisses, and, in October, Agnes surprised the smitten Hemingway by volunteering for duty in Florence, Italy. He wrote to her often, and she answered. Hemingway himself made one abortive trip back to the Italian front, but soon fell ill with jaundice, and had to return to Milan. Seemingly determined to end their relationship, Agnes volunteered at another far-off hospital not long after her work in Florence ended. Finally Hemingway got the message, and in January 1919 he returned to America.

A Soldier's Return

After the excitement of Italy, Agnes, and the Great War, Hemingway rapidly grew bored with civilian life. He had returned home a hero, giving newspaper interviews and speeches to high school assemblies. He limped around Oak Park in a uniform accented by a black cape and a cane, reveling in the romantic status of the wounded war hero. But once the glow of his heroism wore off, everyday life was no substitute. His brush with death and love had irrevocably changed his outlook on life, but back in Oak Park he was no longer a hero but an unemployed son. Adding to his dismay, Agnes, to whom he had still been writing every day, wrote back that she had fallen in love with an Italian lieutenant. Hemingway was devastated, and took to his bed with a fever like the jilted heroine of a romance novel. Writing ultimately eased his despair, though his efforts were still somewhat amateurish and he had yet to develop what would come to be called the Hemingway style. Try as he would, he could not yet effectively translate his war experiences into fiction. The great account of his adventures in Italy, *A Farewell to Arms*, was still a decade away. The Hemingway who could claim that bullets barely hurt and still wished to bask in his heroism was not yet the man who would create the cynical Frederic Henry, a character who, in the novel's most famous passage, shares his embarrassment with the platitudes of patriotism and describes those killed in combat as "meat."

Hemingway also ran into trouble with his parents. Expecting them to treat him as a man who had gone off to war, survived, and returned a minor celebrity, he instead found that Clarence and Grace still regarded him as a boy. He tried to sell his stories to magazines but was greeted only by rejection. Like the hero of his story, "Soldier's Home," which he would later publish in his volume *In Our Time*, Hemingway preferred procrastination to career choice: He would not go to college, get a job, or even make up his bed.

That winter Hemingway made use of a friendship with a wealthy Canadian family to establish contacts that enabled him to submit freelance articles to the *Toronto Star Weekly*. He published his first article on February 14, 1920, and fifteen others in the next few months. The paper was pleased with his work and offered him a position on their daily, but Hemingway declined. By late spring of 1920 he returned to Oak Park, awaiting the annual trip to the Hemingway summer home, Windemere. Hemingway anticipated a lazy summer of fishing. But his parents had other ideas; they expected him to pitch in and share in the daily chores. A letter from Clarence Hemingway suggests the tension between the parents and son:

> Do hope dear Ernest that you will think more of what others have done for you and try to be charitable and kind and gentle.

Do not doubt that I am proud of your ability and independence, but try and soften your temper and never threaten your Father and Mother.

Grace in particular grew frustrated by her son's laziness, and she and Ernest had a series of disputes over alleged minor and major offenses. Just after Hemingway turned twenty-one in the summer of 1920, he and his Red Cross buddy, Ted Brumback, were persuaded by two of Hemingway's younger sisters, Ursula and Sunny, to chaperone a secret midnight outing. When their empty beds were discovered, Ernest took most of the blame for the otherwise innocent adventure. In her own words, Grace Hemingway "told them to pack up all their things and leave."

Marriage and Paris

Hemingway broke from his parents and moved to Chicago. There he made many new friends, among them Sherwood Anderson, an established author who read and admired some of Hemingway's short stories. He encouraged Hemingway to go to Paris, the center of the postwar literary scene, and wrote his friends there about a "young fellow of extraordinary talent."

In November 1920, a mutual friend introduced Hemingway to Hadley Richardson of St. Louis, a tall, auburn-haired woman eight years his senior. He was immediately drawn to her: "I knew she was the girl I was going to marry," he told his brother years later. They were indeed married on September 3, 1921, and honeymooned at Windemere, after a reconciliation with Hemingway's parents.

Following Anderson's advice, Hemingway took his bride to Paris, carrying letters of introduction to several people who would have a dramatic effect on his life and writing career: Lewis Galantiere, an American translator and writer; Ezra Pound, the eccentric poet whose aesthetic genius would influence many of the greatest works of the period; and Gertrude Stein, another boisterous and eccentric writer and patron of the arts who encouraged such artists as Pablo Picasso, Georges Braque, and Henri Matisse. Stein's home at 27 rue de Fleurus was a meeting place for writers, artists, and critics. "If you are lucky enough to have lived in Paris as a young man," Hemingway would later write in a memoir, "then wherever you go for the rest of your life, it stays with you, for Paris is a moveable feast." Postwar Paris was remarkably attractive to the young couple. Besides its burgeoning literary scene, the city offered inexpensive living, and Ernest and Hadley were quite comfortable living off her three-thousand-dollar-a-year trust fund and his salary as European correspondent for the *Toronto Star Weekly*.

Stein and Pound read and liked Hemingway's work, and, bolstered by their positive critiques, he applied himself doggedly to his writing. He revised incessantly, often crossing out what had taken him hours to set down, searching for "one true sentence" upon which to build a piece. He wanted, above all, to hone his craft, to write in a clean, crisp, direct style that eliminated pretension and artificiality. When not pursuing poetry and fiction, he spent time in Sylvia Beach's famous bookstore and lending library, Shakespeare and Company, wrote articles for the *Toronto Star*, and took Hadley on trips around Europe, even revisiting Italy to search for the site where he had been wounded. In November 1922, while he was covering a story in Switzerland for the *Star*, he met Hadley at the train station and discovered her in tears. She calmed herself to tell Hemingway that she had packed up all of his manuscripts, both originals and carbon copies, and lost them at the Paris train station. According to Carlos Baker, that suitcase contained the original draft of the novel *A Farewell to Arms*. Baker writes that this draft

> seems to have been highly romantic in manner and conception. It was also written in a prose style considerably more elaborate and adjectival than the one we customarily associate with the young Hemingway. But this early version of the novel, such as it was, has been missing these forty years [in 1965]. The probabilities are that it long ago dissolved in the waters of a Parisian sewer or went up in flames to kindle someone's kitchen fire in the slums of the capital.

The loss of so much work devastated Hemingway, but soon Hadley had more news: She was pregnant. The couple decided to return to Toronto for the birth of the baby, but Hemingway finished one major project before he left Paris: Robert McAlmon had accepted for publication his first book, *Three Stories and Ten Poems*, and Hemingway worked busily at checking the proofs. When he expressed disappointment at the book's thinness to Gertrude Stein, she suggested that he fatten it up with blank pages and a table of contents. In August 1923, after Hemingway finished proofing the manuscript, he and Hadley sailed for America.

John Hadley Nicanor Hemingway was born on October 11, 1923. He was soon known as Bumby, a nickname that would stay with him into adulthood. Hemingway went back to work for the *Toronto Star*, but he did not get along with the paper's new editor, Harry Hindmarsh, who went out of his way to make life miserable for Hemingway, even sending the reporter to New York when his baby was due. Ernest and Hadley soon decided to return to Paris, and, after a brief visit to Oak Park, sailed for Europe in January 1924.

Hemingway took a part-time, nonpaying position with the *transatlantic review*, a monthly literary magazine run by the novelist Ford Madox Ford. He wrote a number of short stories at this time, including "Indian Camp" and "Big Two-Hearted River," both of which would be included in his collection *In Our Time*, brought out by Boni and Liveright, a New York publishing house, in 1925. The book received some favorable reviews, but Hemingway was not happy to be cast as part of a new "school" of writing that included Gertrude Stein and Sherwood Anderson. He sought to separate himself by penning *The Torrents of Spring*, a parody of Anderson's work. Some biographers think that Hemingway also wrote the novel because he wanted to break free from his publishing house and sign with Scribner's, whose renowned editor Maxwell Perkins also edited F. Scott Fitzgerald. Hemingway knew that Boni and Liveright would not publish *The Torrents of Spring* because it disparaged Anderson, one of their more prominent writers. Once Boni and Liveright rejected *Torrents*, Hemingway was free to sign elsewhere.

THE SUN ALSO RISES

In 1925 Hemingway and Hadley traveled to Pamplona, Spain, to see the running of the bulls and subsequent bullfights, accompanied by a coterie of their friends and acquaintances. The trip was notable for its flirtations, extramarital intrigues, bouts of extended drinking, Hemingway's participation in the running of the bulls, and a near fistfight between Hemingway and Harold Loeb, an independently wealthy magazine editor. Many of these incidents, and almost all of the friends, found their way into Hemingway's next novel, *The Sun Also Rises*, which he wrote during the summer of 1925. Hemingway's attraction to the striking Englishwoman Lady Duff Twysden provided the model for the relationship of reporter Jacob Barnes and Brett Ashley. As Hemingway's infatuation with Twysden subsided, another woman, the glamorous Pauline Pfeiffer, set her sights on the writer. Their affair began in February 1926, and by August Hemingway had left Hadley. He married Pauline in May 1927.

The Sun Also Rises appeared in October 1926, and was an immediate hit with both critics and the public. The first several printings sold out quickly, and soon young women were dressing, talking, and cutting their hair short like Lady Brett Ashley. Suddenly Ernest Hemingway was a celebrity. So too had his financial status abruptly changed. Magazines that formerly sent rejection slips now paid substantial sums to publish stories such as "In Another Country" and "Fifty Grand"; sales from *The Sun Also Rises* continued to be strong; and Pauline's wealthy family supplemented the Hemingways' income.

BIRTH AND DEATH

But again family issues complicated Hemingway's life. Pauline was pregnant, and, like Hadley before her, wanted to have the baby in the United States. Hemingway's friend John Dos Passos had recommended Key West, Florida, as a perfect writer's retreat. As the Hemingways left for America, Ernest was working on a novel, *Jimmy Breen*, and a short story in which he would fictionalize his war experiences in Italy and his love affair with Agnes von Kurowsky. Encountering difficulties with the novel, he was forced to put it aside, but the short story grew and grew. He resumed work on it in March 1928 in his new home in Key West, and soon it was more than ten thousand words long and "going well." The story would eventually blossom into *A Farewell to Arms*.

Hemingway's parents were vacationing in Florida at the time, and when they arrived in Key West in April, Ernest was shocked to see his father's deteriorating condition. Clarence Hemingway, who suffered from diabetes and heart trouble, made a shocking contrast to his robust wife.

Pauline wanted to have her baby in Kansas City, which had first-rate medical facilities, and on June 28, Hemingway's second son, Patrick, was born. As his wife recovered from a difficult labor and Caesarean delivery, Hemingway left for the mountains of Wyoming. Throughout the trip, Hemingway continued working on his book. By August 18, when Pauline and Patrick joined him, he was close to completing the first draft of the still unnamed "Italian" novel. The Hemingways traveled extensively during this period, as Ernest finished his draft and decided on the name *A Farewell to Arms*, after a sixteenth-century poem by the English writer George Peele. At Scribner's, Maxwell Perkins was pleased with his progress, and Hemingway planned to return to Key

West in a few weeks to begin revisions. But on December 6, 1928, he received a telegram that his father had died. When he arrived in Oak Park, he learned that Clarence Hemingway, depressed by his poor health, and fearing amputation of his legs due to the insidious progress of diabetes, had committed suicide with a Civil War pistol.

If Hemingway's wounding in 1918 was the seminal event of his life, Clarence Hemingway's suicide is, arguably, a close second. Noted Hemingway scholar Philip Young speculates that a key to understanding Hemingway appears in the short story "Indian Camp," when Hemingway's fictional alter ego, Nick Adams, accompanies his doctor father, who performs a Caesarean section on a Native American woman with a jackknife and without anesthesia. After the operation is over, the doctor looks in the bunk above the woman's bed, where her invalid husband had been listening to her screams for two days. He has committed suicide.

"Why did he kill himself, Daddy?" Nick Adams asks.

"I don't know, Nick," his father replies. "He couldn't stand things, I guess."

In 1961, suffering from assorted ailments, Hemingway himself would commit suicide. His sister, Ursula, diagnosed with terminal cancer, would do the same in 1962, as would his brother, Leicester, on hearing in 1982, that he, too, would have to lose his legs to diabetes.

A FAREWELL TO ARMS

After the funeral, the Hemingways returned to Key West, where Ernest began the revisions on *A Farewell to Arms*. He worked for six hours a day, usually in the morning, editing first with pencil, then on a typewriter. Hemingway cut major sections of the original draft, as he sought to hone and polish the novel. The process was not easy: "I've had hell's own time writing and worse rewriting it," he wrote.

As a final step, Hemingway turned his thoroughly revised manuscript over to Pauline and his sister Sunny for typing. The revision process took five weeks, and on January 22, 1929, the novel was complete. Hemingway wanted Perkins to come to Key West to pick up the manuscript. Perkins agreed, and on February 1 he arrived in Key West. Biographer Kenneth Lynn suggests that after Dr. Hemingway's death there followed "a deepening of the editorial relationship between Hemingway and Max Perkins into a more personal pact," and that, from this point on, Perkins "assumed a fatherly role" in

Hemingway's life. Each day the two men went fishing from six in the morning until late afternoon. Afterwards, Perkins read the manuscript. He immediately knew that he had a winner.

Perkins's only reservations concerned the novel's coarse language. Seeking a realistic portrayal of soldiers in wartime, Hemingway had included off-color words and sexually frank discussion. Perkins hoped to have *A Farewell to Arms* serialized in *Scribner's Magazine*, and no story with offensive language could be included in a mass-market publication. Nevertheless, when the editor returned to New York, he persuaded Scribner's to pay Hemingway sixteen thousand dollars for rights, a record at the time. The subsequent deletions of sensitive material made by Scribner's editors infuriated Hemingway, and much of his correspondence with his New York editors centered around how much Hemingway would have to cut and what language could be preserved. Hemingway wrote Perkins:

> There has always been first rate writing and then American writing (genteel writing). But you should not go backwards. If a word can be printed and is needed in the text it is a *weakening* to omit it. If it *cannot* be printed without the book being suppressed all right.
>
> No one that has read the Mss. [manuscript] has been shocked by *words*. The words do not stand out unless you put a ring around them.

The reviews were almost unanimous in their praise. One compared the book to Shakespeare's *Romeo and Juliet*. Major critics such as Malcolm Cowley, Clifton Fadiman, Henry Seidel Canby, and Arnold Bennett touted the novel as among the best recently produced. Biographer Kenneth Lynn observes that "a *New Yorker* profile by Dorothy Parker on November 30, 1929, may be said to have marked the point at which Hemingway passed beyond mere fame into living legend." Parker, the celebrated critic and writer known for the caustic wit with which she savaged lesser writers, wrote that her awe for Hemingway rivaled that which a tourist might feel on seeing a sunset over the Grand Canyon.

Hemingway, who like many authors was highly sensitive to the critics, was elated by the accolades. Even so, he maintained a sense of humor about those who did not understand the novel as he meant it. He wrote Perkins:

> I saw in the [newspaper] that some citizen was *lecturing* on Farewell to Arms. God it would be fine to walk in and ask a

few questions and then say "[Expletive], Sir I do believe you are mistaken!"

The novel topped the best-seller list and sold twenty-eight thousand copies in just a few weeks. With part of his windfall, Hemingway established a trust fund for his now-dependent mother, Grace, to whom he had been sending one hundred dollars a month after Clarence Hemingway's death.

Despite the elimination of many foul words and graphic passages, some still found the novel offensive. The Boston superintendent of police banned from city newsstands the June issue of *Scribner's Magazine* containing an installment of *A Farewell to Arms*.

WORLD TRAVELER

In 1931, after renting various places in Key West, the Hemingways settled into their own home on Whitehead Street, a gift from Pauline's uncle Gus. Hemingway continued to write stories and began a new long work, *Death in the Afternoon*, based on his experiences attending bullfights. He made a trip to Spain in the spring and summer of 1931 to gather additional material, and while there observed the mounting political unrest that would soon erupt into civil war. Back in the States, on November 12, 1931, Hemingway's third son, Gregory Hancock Hemingway, was born.

Death in the Afternoon was published in September 1932 to generally favorable reviews. Not long after, Paramount Pictures released a feature film version of *A Farewell to Arms*, starring Gary Cooper and Helen Hayes. Hemingway was not happy to learn that the screenwriters had given the film a happy ending.

Hemingway made fishing trips to Havana, Cuba, a horseback riding excursion in Wyoming, a tour of Spain, and a safari to Africa during these years. Many of his travels were recounted in various short stories and novels. The twenty-five thousand dollar African safari, also financed by Pauline's uncle Gus, generated, among other works, classic short stories such as "The Snows of Kilimanjaro" and "The Short Happy Life of Francis Macomber," and *The Green Hills of Africa*, a slightly fictionalized account of the trip. In the latter work, the character of "Papa," like Nick Adams, Jacob Barnes, and Frederic Henry before him, is clearly modeled on Hemingway, as Hemingway had begun going by the name of "Papa" while he was still in his twenties.

Hemingway embarked on a series of trips to Spain after

civil war broke out there in 1936. He sided solidly with the Spanish Loyalists against Francisco Franco's revolutionaries. Between trips, Hemingway fell in love. His marriage to Pauline had been deteriorating for some time, and when he met an attractive blonde, Martha "Marty" Gellhorn, in Sloppy Joe's bar in Key West, he was smitten. Gellhorn, a correspondent, had also published a novel and a collection of short stories. She had recently returned from Germany, where she had observed firsthand Adolf Hitler's Nazi Party. Her career would be a source of contention for the always macho Hemingway, who would actually view her as a literary competitor.

Feeling that Hemingway was distancing himself and recognizing in Marty Gellhorn's actions some of the same tricks that she had used to pull Hemingway from his first wife, Pauline Hemingway began spending more time away from her husband. She knew that her marriage would soon be ending. Meanwhile, Hemingway retreated to Havana, Cuba, where a community of Spanish exiles had settled and where, he felt, he could write more diligently. He and Marty found an old farmhouse, the Finca Vigia, which appealed to them, and set about renovating it. In 1939 Hemingway began working on a big novel about the war in Spain. Now firmly ensconced in the Finca Vigia, even while Marty was off covering the war in Europe, he churned out forty-three chapters, finishing on July 1, 1940. *For Whom the Bell Tolls* would prove to be his third major novel, and its sales would exceed those of any of Hemingway's previous work. The book's reviews were also extremely strong.

After finishing his novel, Hemingway drove to the American West with Marty. He was in Idaho when his divorce from Pauline came through. Two weeks later, on November 21, 1940, he and Marty were married in Wyoming by a justice of the peace. They returned to Cuba before embarking on a trip to China.

THE FORTIES

The 1940s was a decade in Hemingway's life notable for what he did not do. Now renowned as a writer and increasingly famous as a personality, Hemingway published no major work for ten years after *For Whom the Bell Tolls*. The first half of the decade saw Hemingway eagerly attempting to join the war effort in unconventional ways. Convinced that German submarines were patrolling the Caribbean, Hemingway gained U.S. government approval for a quixotic scheme whereby he would outfit his thirty-eight-foot boat, the *Pilar*, with bazookas, bombs, grenades, and machine guns and stalk the enemy. But only one German sub ever appeared, far off in the distance, and Hemingway never got close to it. Marty, who had remained overseas after their honeymoon trip so that she might continue reporting on the war, had nothing but scorn for Hemingway's war efforts. In retaliation, he criticized her writing, suggesting that she should spend more time as a wife and less as a hack reporter.

By now Hemingway had grown the full beard that would become his trademark. He spent much of his time drinking excessively with friends and devoting precious little effort to writing. He did edit a selection of stories designed to help the war effort, *Men at War*, which was published in 1942 to mixed reviews. His relationship with Marty was souring: She argued continually with him about his drinking, his sloppiness (she referred to him as "the pig"), and his huge ego. But when Marty returned to Europe to cover the war, Hemingway did the same, accepting an offer to write for the magazine *Collier's*. He arrived in London in May 1944 and met and promptly fell for Mary Welsh, a petite, married blonde who worked for *Time* and *Life* magazines.

Hemingway threw himself into the European war effort with the same ardor that had characterized his submarine hunting in the Caribbean. He was present at the D-Day landing at Normandy, though his reports were often inaccurate. He broke the rules of the Geneva Convention by carrying weapons and participating in combat (journalists were not allowed to do either). He distinguished himself among the soldiers and officers, if not among rival and often envious reporters, by his bravery, often under fire. But some of those envious reporters alerted authorities to his unauthorized activities, and he might have been in serious trouble when called before a military inspector. Instead, Hemingway uncharacteristically downplayed his role in combat situations, and numerous other journalists and officers were ready to vouch for him. The charges were dropped.

When World War II ended Hemingway returned to Cuba; he had almost as much trouble adjusting to civilian life as he had had after World War I. In March 1945 he and Marty agreed to divorce. He married Mary a year later. Hemingway had told Maxwell Perkins that he would write a novel based on his war experiences, but the going was slow, and Perkins died in 1947. The novel, *Across the River and into the Trees*, could have used

Perkins's editing magic; and, when it was finally published in 1950, a full decade after his last novel, the critics were harsh. They claimed Hemingway had lost his touch, and that he was too interested in adventure and cultivating friendships with famous people to apply himself seriously to his work.

ONE LAST TRIUMPH

Always subject to bouts of depression, especially when he suffered from writer's block or when the critics pounced on his work, Hemingway nevertheless applied himself to a work of fiction that he had begun years before about a fisherman who loses a magnificent catch to a swarm of ravenous sharks. That novella, *The Old Man and the Sea*, earned Hemingway accolades. Immediately declared an American classic by critics, the book, first published in its entirety in a single issue of *Life* magazine, won the Pulitzer Prize and reestablished Hemingway as one of the premier writers of his time.

In 1953 Hemingway embarked on a second African safari. The trip was filled with adventure, including two airplane crashes in three days. After the first, Hemingway was presumed dead, and obituaries appeared in newspapers around the world, celebrating the life and writings of the great novelist. Hemingway was flattered and fascinated by accounts of his life, but the incidents took an ironic turn. When he was awarded the Nobel Prize in literature for 1954, he wondered whether his presumed death as much as his literary output had accounted for the award.

Recovering from a host of injuries after the plane crashes, Hemingway did not make the trip to Sweden to collect his prize. Instead, he tape-recorded a statement to be played when the American ambassador to Sweden, John Cabot, accepted the award on his behalf. Part of this famous speech sounds more like an apology than a celebration:

> Writing, at its best, is a lonely life. Organizations for writers palliate the writer's loneliness but I doubt if they improve his writing. He grows in public stature as he sheds his loneliness and often his work deteriorates. For he does his work alone and if he is a good enough writer he must face eternity, or the lack of it, each day.

FINAL DAYS

Hemingway slowly recovered from his injuries at the Finca Vigia in Cuba, but new maladies began to plague him, including hypertension and chronic liver malfunction. For the remainder of his life he was never healthy, and he published nothing of significance in his last nine years. The cumulative effects of generally hard living, war wounds, car crashes, and now plane crashes had taken their toll. Philip Young summarizes Hemingway's injuries in this way:

> His skull was fractured at least once; he sustained at least a dozen brain concussions, several of them serious ones; he was in three bad automobile accidents; and [as a result of his two plane accidents] . . . he suffered severe internal injuries, "jammed" his spine, and received a concussion so violent that his eyesight was impaired for some time. . . . In warfare alone he was shot through nine parts of his body, and sustained six head wounds.

In fact, Hemingway's friend, the writer John Dos Passos, once remarked that he had never known an athletic man who spent more time in bed due to illness and injury than Hemingway. Along with his most recent maladies, Hemingway's old bouts with depression returned. He did manage to write a memoir of his days in Paris in the twenties, replete with accounts of F. Scott Fitzgerald, Gertrude Stein, Ezra Pound, and others, which would be published posthumously as *A Moveable Feast*. But in 1959 his life was further disrupted when Fidel Castro successfully rebelled against the Batista regime in Cuba. Fearing the turmoil that would follow the revolution, Hemingway purchased a chalet-style house outside of Ketchum, Idaho, in March 1959.

Hemingway's depression deepened. He began another work, this time on bullfighting, and made a final trip to the country that was near to his heart, Spain. The record of that trip would be published posthumously as *The Dangerous Summer*. But mostly he felt run down and battered by a lifetime of hard living and hard writing. "I'm bone-tired and very beat-up emotionally," he told his friend A.E. Hotchner. His liver was enlarged, perhaps from excessive drinking; he displayed symptoms of diabetes and his blood pressure was elevated. He suffered from insomnia, loneliness, and paranoia. Refusing psychotherapy, Hemingway admitted himself to the Mayo Clinic in Rochester, Minnesota, known for its discretion in caring for distinguished patients. He endured numerous treatments of shock therapy, which was believed at the time to help relieve depression and other psychological illnesses. Back in Idaho he tried to resume his lifelong early morning writing schedule, but the words would not come. On the morning of July 2, 1961, he selected a double-barreled shotgun from his collection and shot himself in the head.

Characters and Plot

The Characters

Frederic Henry. The narrator, Frederic is a disillusioned young army lieutenant, an American serving in the Italian ambulance unit. He spends his free time drinking, carousing, and womanizing, though he is aware that life can offer more than the meaningless pursuit of pleasure. Nevertheless, it is not until he meets and subsequently falls in love with Catherine Barkley that he begins, almost despite himself, to become more serious about life.

Catherine Barkley. A beautiful army v.a.d. (volunteer aide), she is tall and blonde with "tawny skin and gray eyes." Catherine has lost a former lover to warfare. She is sentimental and fragile when she first meets Frederic. She soon falls in love with him. Catherine is not a profound thinker, but she enjoys life, especially her time with Frederic. She worries about the future and the consequences of their relationship. She faces difficult situations, including her pregnancy, with great stoicism. Catherine dies in childbirth at the end of the novel.

Rinaldi. An army surgeon, Rinaldi is Frederic's friend and roommate. He is a mercurial, cynical jokester who counters the horrors of war and the many operations he must perform on terribly wounded soldiers with a hedonistic, live-for-pleasure attitude. He is a womanizer who meets and dates Catherine Barkley prior to introducing her to Frederic. When Frederic last encounters Rinaldi, the surgeon is a pathetic, worn-out man who fears he has contracted syphilis from his philandering.

The Priest. A nameless young Italian army chaplain, he counsels Frederic to look for the more spiritual side of life. Love, he tells Frederic, is the willingness to sacrifice oneself for others, not a selfish pursuit of pleasure. The Priest is subjected to much teasing and obscene language by the other officers, but he maintains his dignity and never stoops to their level by responding in kind. "In my country," he tells Frederic, "it is understood that a man may love God. It is not a dirty joke."

Helen Ferguson. A Scottish nurse, she is Catherine's co-worker and best friend. She is a woman of strong morals who disapproves of Frederic; she believes he is only using Catherine. Nevertheless she is very loyal and aids Catherine in any way that she can.

Ettore Moretti. An Italian from San Francisco who serves in the Italian army, he loves war and its rewards. He has been wounded badly three times, for which he wears three "wound stripes" on his uniform sleeve. He has also earned two bronze and three silver medals. "He's the boy they're running the war for," one of the characters jokes. He is quick to brag about his wounds and show them off. According to Frederic, Ettore "was a legitimate hero who bored everyone he met."

Count Greffi. A ninety-four-year-old retired diplomat, he has white hair and a mustache and "beautiful manners." Greffi and Frederic play billiards, drink, and engage in serious conversation. Greffi is a more gentle cynic than Rinaldi or Frederic and believes that love, not cynicism, can sustain one in the most difficult of times.

THE PLOT

Set on the Italian front during World War I, *A Farewell to Arms* is the story of American lieutenant Frederic Henry, who has enlisted in the Italian ambulance corps. Having signed up for no particular reason ("I was in Italy . . . and I spoke Italian," he tells a nurse), Frederic shows no allegiance to any person, cause, or country. Morally he is dissolute, spending his free time drinking with fellow officers or patronizing the local bordello. With the approach of winter and a corresponding lull in combat, Frederic takes leave. His fellow officers suggest he go to the cities where he can drink and meet women, while the young priest who serves his unit suggests he go on a sort of spiritual retreat to the priest's home in the Abruzzi mountains. After his return, we learn that the morally lax young American has opted for the cities, much to the disappointment of the priest.

It is spring, and a new offensive is about to commence. In preparation, a group of British nurses has arrived at the front. Frederic's friend and roommate, a cynical, hard-drinking Italian surgeon named Rinaldi, takes Frederic to meet the nurses, including his own favorite, a tall, blonde, very beautiful woman named Catherine Barkley. Frederic is immediately attracted to Barkley, but when he tries to kiss her during their first meeting, she slaps him. Only moments later, she lets the angry and embarrassed Frederic kiss her. Then she breaks into tears, telling him, "We're going to have a strange life." Despite his belief that Catherine is "probably a little crazy," Frederic returns to see her, ready to promise anything to gain her affections. When Catherine asks, "You did say you loved me, didn't you?" Frederic says he does, but allows the reader to know that he lied. "This was a game, like bridge," Frederic tells us, "in which you said things instead of playing cards. Like bridge you had to pretend you were playing for money or playing for some stakes." Though Catherine shares Frederic's belief that their flirtation is merely a game, she gives him a St. Anthony medal for luck just before he is to leave for the front.

The Italian offensive against the Austrians resumes. One night, while Frederic is sharing a meal with his fellow ambulance drivers, an enemy mortar shell explodes in their dugout. "Through the other noise I heard a cough, then came the chuh-chuh-chuh-chuh—then there was a flash, as when a blast-furnace door is swung open, and a roar that started white and went red and on and on in a rushing wind." One man dies when his legs are blown off, and Frederic is severely wounded in the legs and head. The other ambulance drivers carry him to safety, but not without dropping him, as shells continue to land around them. Later, as Frederic is transported to a field hospital by ambulance, a gruesome incident transpires. The man in the bunk above him hemorrhages, and the blood oozes down onto Frederic, who is nearly helpless to avoid the sticky spill.

At the field hospital, Frederic has two visitors, first Rinaldi and later the young priest. Rinaldi assures Frederic that he will be decorated for bravery, perhaps with a silver medal, at least with a bronze. Frederic is not interested and truthfully insists that his was not an act of bravery. "I was blown up while we were eating cheese," he explains. Promising to send for Catherine Barkley, Rinaldi leaves. Frederic and the priest share a drink and discuss religion and love. "When you love you wish to do things for," the priest says. "You wish to sacrifice for. You wish to serve." "I don't love," Frederic responds.

When he is able to travel, Frederic is taken to a newly installed hospital in Milan. He is the first patient; even the doctors have not yet arrived. Frederic meets several nurses, including the young, friendly Miss Gage, and Miss Van Campen, the superintendent, an older woman of whom he says, "She did not like me and I did not like her. She was small and neatly suspicious and too good for her position." Miss Van Campen forbids Frederic from drinking wine unless the doctor prescribes it, but Frederic bribes a porter to bring him a continual supply, which he hides first behind his bed and later in the room's armoire.

The next day Catherine Barkley arrives; she has been reassigned to the hospital. Frederic realizes that he has fallen in love with her. "God knows I had not wanted to fall in love with her. I had not wanted to fall in love with anyone. But God knows I had."

That afternoon the doctor arrives. He inspects Frederic's leg and decides that surgery will have to be delayed for six months, until the leg has healed sufficiently. Believing that he would go stir crazy in bed for a half-year, Frederic requests a second opinion. Another surgeon, Dr. Valentini, soon arrives. He shares a drink with Frederic, inspects the wound, and declares that he will operate in the morning.

That night Catherine and Frederic make love in his hospital bed. Following Dr. Valentini's successful operation, the two spend the summer together as Frederic recuperates in the hospital. Catherine visits Frederic in his room nightly, and works diligently at her other nursing duties to make sure that the head nurse can find nothing to criticize. During the days, they dine in quiet restaurants and take carriage rides in the park. On one occasion, they go to the racetrack and bet on the horses. When Frederic suggests that they get married, Catherine declines. "We are married privately," she says.

As his recovery progresses, Frederic moves around first on crutches and later with a cane. He undergoes physical therapy, though the range of motion of his injured leg continues to be limited. One evening in late summer, Catherine and Frederic sit alone on a balcony as it begins to rain. Catherine admits she is afraid of the rain. When Frederic badgers her to reveal why, she replies, "I'm afraid of the rain because sometimes I see me dead in it."

The fall approaches, and Frederic must soon leave to return to the front. First, though, he receives a three-week convalescent leave. He makes plans to spend his leave with Catherine, who reveals that she is almost three months pregnant. Before they can depart for their chosen vacation spot of

Pallanza on Lago (Lake) Maggiore, Frederic comes down with jaundice. The head nurse discovers the stash of empty wine and liquor bottles in Frederic's armoire and accuses him of using alcohol to bring on his disease and avoid returning to active duty. She reports him to the authorities, and Frederic's convalescent leave is revoked. Frederic and Catherine spend a final night together in a hotel room. Catherine bravely assures Frederic that all will go well with the baby: "We may have several babies before the war is over," she tells him. They say goodbye in the rain.

Back at the front, Frederic finds that morale is lower than ever. Even the mercurial Rinaldi is depressed at not having enough patients. His work is his life, which is otherwise meaningless and filled with escapades of drinking and carousing. He suspects he may have contracted syphilis. Rinaldi teases Frederic about looking like a married man, then inspects his leg and pronounces the operation a success. He suggests that Frederic should have been given more physical therapy before returning, however. The priest, too, is depressed by the interminable war. "It has been a terrible summer," he tells Frederic.

Frederic learns that the Germans have reinforced the enemy Austrian troops along the front, and that the Italian army is preparing a general retreat from Caporetto. Frederic and his fellow drivers join in the withdrawal, driving south in ambulances loaded with hospital equipment. Along the way, they pick up two Italian girls and two sergeants who have fallen behind. Finding the main roads jammed with peasants, wagons, troops, and trucks, Frederic opts for the back roads. But his truck becomes lodged in deep mud, and the two sergeants, ignoring Frederic's repeated orders to help push the vehicle, set off down the road on foot. Frederic takes out his pistol, and brings down one of the insubordinate men; the other escapes into the night.

Frederic and his three ambulance drivers, Aymo, Piani, and Bonello, abandon their vehicles and set out on foot. Attempting to avoid the enemy, the men are mistakenly fired on by their own army. Aymo is shot in the head and dies almost immediately. The remaining three men hide in a barn until it is safe to continue. Fearing for his life, Bonello leaves, determined to save his life by surrendering to the enemy. Frederic and the loyal Piani join a mob of Italian soldiers heading for the bridge across the Tagliamento River. There are rumors that some Germans have donned Italian uniforms and are posing as Italian officers. On the other side of the bridge, Italian carabiniere, or military police, have been arresting officers. Frederic is apprehended and roughly pulled aside for interrogation. He realizes that after questioning the officers, the carabiniere kill them. Seizing an opportunity, Frederic dashes off and dives into the river. The carabiniere fire on him, but when he finally comes up for air, he is safe in the dark, icy river.

Frederic jumps aboard a train bound for Milan, hiding underneath a tarp in a freight car loaded with ammunition. In Milan, he returns to the hospital where he had been a patient. Learning that Catherine has left for Stresa, he borrows civilian clothing from a friend and buys a train ticket for Stresa. He is saddened that he can no longer return to the army, and that he will not see Rinaldi or the priest again. He has made "a separate peace." In Stresa he finds Catherine on leave with her friend and fellow nurse, Helen Ferguson. "Fergy" berates Frederic for getting Catherine pregnant, calling him a "dirty sneaking American Italian." She cries and then admits that she wants the couple to be happy. Frederic and Catherine share a pleasant interlude in Stresa, and there Frederic meets ninety-four-year-old Count Greffi. As the two play billiards in the hotel, Greffi imparts to Frederic his philosophy of life. Greffi is a Hemingway code hero, a man who believes in living well and honestly despite the hardships he may encounter.

That night, the hotel barman awakens Frederic to warn him that he is to be arrested in the morning as a deserting officer in the morning. The barman gives Frederic a rowboat, and he and Catherine set out across Lake Maggiore, hoping to escape to Switzerland. By morning, Frederic's hands are so raw from rowing that he can barely touch the oars. Frederic and Catherine arrive safely in Switzerland, but are arrested by Swiss customs. Frederic concocts an elaborate tale, explaining that they are cousins who have come to Switzerland for the winter sports. The customs agents, impressed that Frederic and Catherine are carrying a large sum of money, forget about detaining the couple and instead bicker about the best Swiss town in which to enjoy winter sports.

The couple spend a joyous fall and winter in a picturesque Swiss chalet overlooking Montreux. They walk in the woods and play cards, and Frederic grows a beard. Their worries are few. Frederic again asks Catherine to marry him, but she is visibly pregnant and wishes to wait until after the baby is born.

As the time for Catherine's delivery approaches, they leave Montreux for the hospital at Lausanne. Catherine's labor is extended, and she suffers severe pain, for which the doctors offer anesthesia. Hours pass and there is no progress, so the doctors and Frederic decide on a cesarean section. But their baby son is stillborn, having possibly been choked to death when the umbilical cord wrapped around his neck. The nurses send Frederic out to get some food. When he returns Catherine suffers a series of hemorrhages. Frederic goes into her room and stays with her until she dies. Wishing to say a private good-bye to Catherine, he orders the nurses from the room. But "it wasn't any good. It was like saying goodbye to a statue." Having lost his lover and his child, Frederic walks back to the hotel, alone, in the rain.

CHAPTER 1

Background to *A Farewell to Arms*

The Writing of the Novel

Jeffrey Meyers

According to Hemingway biographer Jeffrey Meyers, despite the similarities in Frederic Henry's life and Hemingway's own, *A Farewell to Arms* should not be taken as a literal record of Hemingway's wartime activities. Hemingway believed in "inventing from knowledge," that is, altering real-life events to make more powerful fiction. Hemingway felt he needed to distance himself from the powerful real-life events of the Great War, and so he did not write the story for a decade. He revised the novel extensively, writing more than thirty versions of the ending alone. Jeffrey Meyers is the author of numerous books, including biographies of Robert Frost, Lawrence of Arabia, and D.H. Lawrence.

In his Introduction to the crudely illustrated 1948 edition of *A Farewell to Arms*, Hemingway described the travels and emotional events that took place during the composition of the novel . . . :

> The book was written in Paris, France, Key West, Florida, Piggott, Arkansas, Kansas City, Missouri, Sheridan, Wyoming, and the first draft of it was finished near Big Horn in Wyoming. It was begun in the last winter months of 1928 and the first draft was finished in September of that year. It was rewritten in the fall and winter of 1928 in Key West and the final writing was finished in Paris in the spring of 1929.
>
> During the time I was writing the first draft my second son Patrick was delivered in Kansas City by Caesarean section and while I was rewriting my father killed himself in Oak Park, Illinois. I was not quite thirty years old when I finished the book and the day it was published was the day [sic] the stock market crashed.

The novel exemplifies Hemingway's theory of inventing from knowledge, his belief that an author must have some

---

Excerpted from *Hemingway: A Biography*, by Jeffrey Meyers. Copyright © 1985 by Jeffrey Meyers. Reprinted with the permission of HarperCollins Publishers, Inc.

actual experience though not necessarily the precise experience of what he writes about. To illustrate this idea, he contrasted [Russian novelist Leo] Tolstoy's memoir of the Crimean War with his fictional description of Napoleonic battles in *War and Peace*: "Dr. Tolstoi was at Sevastopol. But not at Borodino. He wasn't in business in those days. But he could invent from knowledge. We were all at some damned Sevastopol." And in a letter to his French translator, Maurice Coindreau, he emphasized the imaginative rather than the autobiographical elements of the novel, discounted his service in Italy and did not even mention his war wound. He refused to furnish biographical or military material because the publishers used it to make his novel seem a "document." And he forbade Scribner's to use personal publicity because he wanted his work to be judged purely as fiction.

Hemingway was defensive about documentation because he employed the methods of Tolstoy and [American author of *The Red Badge of Courage*] Stephen Crane to recreate the realistic battle scenes. In *A Farewell to Arms*, the only novel set on terrain which Hemingway did not actually visit, he used military histories and newspaper accounts to provide the factual basis of the Austro-Italian campaigns that took place when the novelist was still in high school in Oak Park. His account of the disastrous defeat in October 1917, when the Austrians, with the help of German troops released from the Russian front after the Revolution, launched an attack on Caporetto, broke the Italian line and hurled it back to the Piave, was so painfully convincing that [Italian dictator Benito] Mussolini's government banned the novel, which was not published in Italy until after World War Two. Frederic Henry's military failure "is the epitome of the general performance of the Italian Second Army during the retreat" and the book accurately reflects the principal causes of the defeat: the Socialist revolt in Turin, the severe shortage of food, the effective enemy propaganda and the poor Italian leadership. . . .

Hemingway told [American novelist] Sinclair Lewis that he could not write about anything until a long time after the event. During the decade between his war experience and the composition of the book, he moved from the youthful idealism expressed in the letters sent from the Milan hospital to the bitter disillusionment portrayed in the great scenes of the novel: the wounding of Frederic, the retreat from Caporetto, the escape into the river, the rowing up Lake Maggiore into

Switzerland, the account of ants swarming toward destruction on a burning log and the death of Catherine in childbirth.

Harold Loeb's observation that Hemingway "distrusted abstractions and intangibles" and put her faith in concrete

An Earlier Ending to *A Farewell to Arms*

Hemingway once told an interviewer that he revised the conclusion to A Farewell to Arms *thirty-nine times (although Jeffrey Meyers claims that the figure is thirty-two). This early ending contained more details about the aftermath of the events in Italy. Hemingway's renowned editor, Maxwell Perkins, found fault with this ending ("It is better not to have gone beyond the end of the story in speaking about Rinaldi, etc."), but did regret Hemingway's cutting of "that terribly poignant line about waking up in the morning and finding everything the same as ever."*

It seems she had one hemorrhage after another. They couldn't stop it.

I went into the room and stayed with Catherine until she died. She was unconscious all the time, and it did not take her very long to die.

There are a great many more details, starting with my first meeting with an undertaker, and all the business of burial in a foreign country and going on with the rest of my life—which has gone on and seems likely to go on for a long time.

I could tell how Rinaldi was cured of the syphilis and lived to find that the technic learned in wartime surgery is not of much practical use in peace. I could tell how the priest in our mess lived to be a priest in Italy under Fascism. I could tell how Ettore became a Fascist and the part he took in that organization. I could tell how Piani got to be a taxi-driver in New York and what sort of a singer Simmons became. Many things have happened. Everything blunts and the world keeps on. It never stops. It only stops for you. Some of it stops while you are still alive. The rest goes on and you go on with it.

I could tell you what I have done since March, nineteen hundred and eighteen, when I walked that night in the rain back to the hotel where Catherine and I had lived and went upstairs to our room and undressed and slept finally, because I was so tired—to wake in the morning with the sun shining in the window; then suddenly to realize what had happened. I could tell what has happened since then, but that is the end of the story.

Carlos Baker, ed., *Ernest Hemingway: Critiques of the Four Major Novels.* New York: Scribner's, 1962, p. 75.

reality is confirmed in *A Farewell to Arms* when Frederic states: "I was always embarrassed by the words sacred, glorious, and sacrifice and the expression in vain. . . . Abstract words such as glory, honor, courage, or hallow were obscene beside the concrete names of villages, the numbers of roads, the names of rivers, the numbers of regiments and the dates." The abstractions were lies; only the actual places where men had fought and died had any dignity and meaning. Another thematic passage—which foreshadows Catherine's fate—expresses Hemingway's pessimistic but stoic response to a malign universe: "If people bring so much courage to this world the world has to kill them to break them, so of course it kills them. The world breaks every one and afterward many are strong at the broken places. But those that will not break it kills. It kills the very good and the very gentle and the very brave impartially. If you are none of these you can be sure it will kill you too but there will be no special hurry."

Frederic Henry participates in the retreat from Caporetto rather than in the redemptive battle of Vittorio Veneto, which occurred exactly one year later and led to the surrender of Austria, in order to represent—like the autobiographical heroes of Robert Graves' *Goodbye to All That*, Richard Aldington's *Death of a Hero* and Erich Remarque's *All Quiet on the Western Front* (all published in 1929)—the destruction of idealism in the war.

The manuscript revisions of *A Farewell to Arms* show that Hemingway was a good self-critic and nearly always improved his early drafts. He drew up a list of thirty-four possible titles, mainly from the Bible and the *Oxford Book of English Verse*, and finally chose one from the Renaissance poet George Peele. He wrote thirty-two versions of the end of the novel, which clearly gave him the most trouble, and wisely omitted a conclusion that sourly and ponderously surveyed the fate of the surviving characters.

THE CRITICAL REACTION

Scribner's Magazine paid Hemingway an unprecedented $16,000 for the serial rights of *A Farewell to Arms*, which he dedicated to Gus Pfeiffer. The June issue was banned in Boston because of immoral episodes and objectionable language, but the unsavory publicity merely intensified the public's interest in the book and increased the substantial sales. Critics felt that Hemingway had achieved a new maturity and depth. The novel received even more praise than his earlier works and in 1929 brought him to the pinnacle of his reputation.

Malcolm Cowley, one of Hemingway's greatest admirers, discussed the extra-literary reasons for his sudden fame: his distance from the jealousies of the New York literary world, his personal legend, his artistic pride, his use of sensational material, his ability to express the viewpoint of his postwar contemporaries. And he saw a new tenderness and seriousness in Hemingway's second novel: "The emotions as a whole are more colored by thought; perhaps they are weaker and certainly they are becoming more complicated. They seem to demand expression in a subtler and richer prose." In [the magazine] *The Criterion* of April 1933 [poet and critic] T.S. Eliot refuted the criticism that Hemingway was both hard-boiled and sentimental, and defended him as a writer who expressed his truest feelings: "The illusion which pervades the whole various-climated American continent is the illusion of the hard-boiled. Even Mr. Ernest Hemingway—the writer of tender sentiment, and true sentiment, as in 'The Killers' and *A Farewell to Arms* . . . has been taken as the representative of the hard-boiled. . . . Mr. Hemingway is a writer for whom I have considerable respect; he seems to me to tell the truth about his own feelings at the moment when they exist." J.B. Priestley, in his literary puff for Jonathan Cape's house magazine, noticed that the characteristically modern lovers "seem to be curiously lonely, without backgrounds, unsustained by any beliefs," and that this somehow adds, to the "terrible poignancy and force" of the concluding scene. . . .

FAREWELL ON STAGE AND SCREEN

Hemingway had less success with the stage and film versions of the novel. It was adapted by Laurence Stallings, opened at the National Theater in New York on September 22, 1930, and ran for only twenty-four performances. In December 1931 the play was produced at the Deutsches Theater in Berlin. Hemingway received $24,000 for the film rights, but thought "The movies ruined everything. Like talking about something good." He hated the screen version of *A Farewell to Arms*, made in 1932 with Gary Cooper and Helen Hayes, and condemned the fake morality, lack of plausibility and the happy ending as well as the absurdity of the phony marriage ceremony, Rinaldi's incredible withholding of letters, and Frederic Henry's inexplicable desertion from the army. He sent a violent but futile protest in a cablegram to Hollywood and wondered if anyone, after seeing such a terrible film, would ever want to read his book. But the first printing of 31,000 copies had doubled by January 1929, and the novel had sold 1,400,000 copies by 1961.

The Euphemistic Language of World War I

Paul Fussell

In his National Book Award–winning study of World War I, *The Great War and Modern Memory*, Paul Fussell depicts the innocence with which soldiers entered into the war. Because there had been no great European wars for almost fifty years, most people had no conception of the harsh realities of combat. Their idea of war was informed by nineteenth-century writers who romanticized warfare and whose language skirted reality in favor of idealizing notions of nobility and valor. After World War I, such delicacy and innocence was impossible. Paul Fussell has taught at the University of Pennsylvania. His many books include *Poetic Meter and Poetic Form* and *Ethics and Imagery from Swift to Burke*.

One reason the Great War was more ironic than any other is that its beginning was more innocent. "Never such innocence again," observes [English poet] Philip Larkin, who has found himself curiously drawn to regard with a wondering tenderness not the merely victimized creatures of the nearby Second World War but the innocents of the remote Great War, those sweet, generous people who pressed forward and all but solicited their own destruction. In "MCMXIV," written in the early sixties, Larkin contemplates a photograph of the patient and sincere lined up in early August outside a recruiting station:

> Those long uneven lines
> Standing as patiently
> As if they were stretched outside
> The Oval or Villa Park,
> The crowns of hats, the sun
> On moustached archaic faces
> Grinning as if it were all
> An August Bank Holiday lark. . . .

Excerpted from *The Great War and Modern Memory*, by Paul Fussell. Copyright © 1975 by Oxford University Press, Inc. Reprinted by permission of Oxford University Press, Inc. Larkin poem: Excerpted from "The Whitsun Weddings," from *The Collected Poems*, by Philip Larkin. Copyright © 1988, 1989 by the Estate of Philip Larkin. Reprinted by permission of Farrar, Straus & Giroux, Inc., and Faber & Faber Ltd.

The shops are shut, and astonishingly, the Defense of the
Realm Act not yet having been thought of,
> ... the pubs
> Wide open all day. . . .

The class system is intact and purring smoothly:
> The differently-dressed servants
> With tiny rooms in huge houses,
> The dust behind limousines. . . .

"Never such innocence," he concludes:
> Never before or since,
> As changed itself to past
> Without a word—the men
> Leaving the gardens tidy,
> The thousands of marriages
> Lasting a little while longer:
> Never such innocence again.

INNOCENCE LOST

Far now from such innocence, instructed in cynicism and draft-dodging by the virtually continuous war since 1936, how can we forbear condescending to the eager lines at the recruiting stations or smiling at news like this, from the *Times* of August 9, 1914:

> At an inquest on the body of Arthur Sydney Evelyn Annesley, aged 49, formerly a captain in the Rifle Brigade, who committed suicide by flinging himself under a heavy van at Pimlico, the Coroner stated that worry caused by the feeling that he was not going to be accepted for service led him to take his life.

But our smiles are not appropriate, for that was a different world. The certainties were intact. Britain had not known a major war for a century, and on the Continent [of Europe], as [historian] A.J.P. Taylor points out, "there had been no war between the Great Powers since 1871. No man in the prime of life knew what war was like. All imagined that it would be an affair of great marches and great battles, quickly decided."

Furthermore, the Great War was perhaps the last to be conceived as taking place within a seamless, purposeful "history" involving a coherent stream of time running from past through present to future. The shrewd recruiting poster depicting a worried father of the future being asked by his children, "Daddy, what did *you* do in the Great War?" assumes a future whose moral and social pressures are identical with those of the past. Today, when each day's experience seems notably *ad hoc*, no such appeal would shame the most stupid to the recruiting office. But the Great War took place in what was, compared with ours, a static world, where the values appeared stable and where the meanings of abstractions seemed permanent and reliable. Everyone knew what Glory was, and what Honor meant. It was not until eleven years after the war that Hemingway could declare in *A Farewell to Arms* that "abstract words such as glory, honor, courage, or hallow were obscene beside the concrete names of villages, the numbers of roads, the names of rivers, the numbers of regiments and the dates." In the summer of 1914 no one would have understood what on earth he was talking about.

THE EUPHEMISTIC LANGUAGE OF WAR

Certainly the author of a personal communication in the *Times* two days before the declaration of war would not have understood:

> PAULINE—Alas, it cannot be. But I will dash into the great venture with all that pride and spirit an ancient race has given me....

The language is that which two generations of readers had been accustomed to associate with the quiet action of personal control and Christian self-abnegation ("sacrifice"), as well as with more violent actions of aggression and defense. The tutors in this special diction had been the boys' books of George Alfred Henty; the male-romances of Rider Haggard; the poems of Robert Bridges; and especially the Arthurian poems of [English poet Alfred, Lord] Tennyson and the pseudo-medieval romances of [English poet] William Morris. We can set out this "raised," essentially feudal language in a table of equivalents:

A friend is a	*comrade*
Friendship is	*comradeship,* or *fellowship*
A horse is a	*steed,* or *charger*
The enemy is	*the foe,* or *the host*
Danger is	*peril*
To conquer is to	*vanquish*
To attack is to	*assail*

To be earnestly brave is to be	*gallant*
To be cheerfully brave is to be	*plucky*
To be stolidly brave is to be	*staunch*
Bravery considered after the fact is	*valor*
The dead on the battlefield are	*the fallen*
To be nobly enthusiastic is to be	*ardent*
To be unpretentiously enthusiastic is to be	*keen*
The front is	*the field*
Obedient soldiers are	*the brave*
Warfare is	*strife*
Actions are	*deeds*
To die is to	*perish*
To show cowardice is to	*swerve*
The draft-notice is	*the summons*
To enlist is to	*join the colors*
Cowardice results in	*dishonor*
Not to complain is to be	*manly*
To move quickly is to be	*swift*
Nothing is	*naught*
Nothing but is	*naught, save*
To win is to	*conquer*
One's chest is one's	*breast*
Sleep is	*slumber*
The objective of an attack is	*the goal*
A soldier is a	*warrior*
One's death is one's	*fate*
The sky is	*the heavens*
Things that glow or shine are	*radiant*
The army as a whole is	*the legion*
What is contemptible is	*base*
The legs and arms of young men are	*limbs*
Dead bodies constitute	*ashes,* or *dust*
The blood of young men is	*"the red/Sweet wine of youth"*
	—R. Brooke.

This system of "high" diction was not the least of the ultimate casualties of the war. But its staying power was astonishing. As late as 1918 it was still possible for some men who had actually fought to sustain the old rhetoric.

Chapter 2
Characters in *A Farewell to Arms*

The Role of Catherine Barkley

Peter L. Hays

Catherine Barkley's role in *A Farewell to Arms* has been a controversial subject since the novel's publication. Though many critics see her as a paper doll figure, an equal number regard her as heroic. Peter L. Hays weighs in with those who find Catherine an impressive woman whose limitations stem from the horrors of serving as a wartime nurse. Her maturity and dedication allow Frederic Henry to grow as a person and to learn the true meaning of love. Peter L. Hays is the author of *The Limping Hero* and *Ernest Hemingway* and has been a board member of the Ernest Hemingway Society. He has taught at the University of California, Davis.

The female protagonist of Ernest Hemingway's *A Farewell to Arms* has received mixed reviews from critics over the years, being seen as compliant, lacking any strong sense of self by some, and heroic by others. One can easily find a dozen critics split equally. Edmund Wilson, in 1941, leads the list of detractors, speaking of Catherine's "abject devotion" to Lt. Henry. Leslie Fiedler described Hemingway's women characters in 1966 as "mindless, soft, subservient; painless devices for extracting seed without human engagement." Philip Young characterized Catherine as "idealized past the fondest belief of most people, and even the more realistic wishes of some, compliant." Wendy Martin sees her thus: "Catherine Barkley is the subservient, compliant companion par excellence: as nurse-mistress to Frederic Henry, she is passive femininity incarnate." The most rabid anti-Hemingway comments come from Judith Fetterley, who says that *A Farewell to Arms* displays hostility toward women and that Catherine's "death is the logical consequence of the cumula-

Excerpted from Peter L. Hays, "Ministrant Barkley in *A Farewell to Arms*," in *Hemingway in Italy and Other Essays*, Robert L. Lewis, ed. Copyright © 1990 by The Ernest Hemingway Foundation. All rights reserved. Reproduced with permission from Greenwood Publishing Group, Inc., Westport, CT. (In-text references and endnotes in the original have been omitted in this reprint.)

tive hostilities Frederic feels toward her." And most recently, in 1984, Millicent Bell described Catherine as "a sort of inflated rubber woman available at will to the onanistic [self-pleasuring] dreamer," Frederic Henry.

THE HEROIC CATHERINE

In contrast to these damning appraisals, Delbert Wylder sees Catherine as the heroine of *A Farewell to Arms*, Jackson Benson describes her as the one who teaches Frederic Henry to love, Deborah Fisher praises her as "the strongest and smartest" of Hemingway's loving women, and Michael Reynolds, like Wylder, elevates Catherine to the novel's main role. Roger Whitlow calls her devotion noble, and Joyce Wexler, whose reading is very close to my own, says that Catherine, when acceding to Frederic's open-mouth kiss, "is not responding to the power of Frederic's lips but to her own resolution to resume her life in spite of her loss. She devises a kind of therapy for herself by pretending to love Frederic in place of her fiancé." Wexler continues:

> Far from being a blind romantic, she is a shellshocked victim of the war who chooses love as a method of rechanneling self-destructive feelings of guilt and remorse.
>
> Just as Frederic joins the Italian army because he is in Italy, Catherine chooses to love him because he is there.
>
> She insists that love depends on the will to love.

I believe that Catherine is not the hero in the sense of being the protagonist—she is absent for long passages—but that she is the code hero of this novel: the embodiment of admirable qualities and Henry's tutor in committing to life and love.

A DEFINITION OF LOVE

Certain details of the relationship between Catherine and Henry have been well discussed, but let me briefly review them. The priest tells Frederic that "When you love you wish to do things for. You wish to sacrifice for. You wish to serve." Frederic makes it obvious that heretofore he has not loved:

> "Have you ever loved any one?" [Catherine asks.]
> "No," . . . [Frederic replies.]
> "I don't love."

He also makes it clear that his initial interest in Catherine is sexual only; he is seeking no commitment:

> [Catherine:] "You did say you loved me, didn't you?"
> [Frederic:] "Yes," I lied. "I love you." I had not said it before. . . .

I thought she was probably a little crazy. It was all right if she was. I did not care what I was getting into. . . . I knew I did not love Catherine Barkley nor had any idea of loving her. This was a game.

A number of critics see Catherine as teaching Frederic to love. Certainly, after her appearance in the hospital in Milan, he repeatedly confesses his love:

> When I saw her I was in love with her. Everything turned over inside of me.
>
> God knows I had not wanted to fall in love with her. . . . But God knows I had.

Moreover, we see him fulfilling the priest's definition of love: doing for, serving. He accompanies Cat on her rounds, carrying bedpans for her, and though it may be argued that in doing so he reduces the time she has to spend with other patients and so increases her time with him, still, it is a service. In Lausanne Frederic reverses roles, nursing Catherine as she had done for him in Milan, even donning a hospital gown as he administers anesthetic from a gas cylinder. But he also serves her in providing a love object, a focus for her self-prescribed romance therapy that cures her unstable mental state and does bring her happiness (short-lived, but certainly longer than Francis Macomber enjoys).

CATHERINE'S NEUROSES

When he meets her, Catherine is, in Frederic's opinion and her own, crazy. Both Norman Grebstein and Wexler attribute her neuroses to guilt over having denied sexual relations to her now-dead fiancé, much like Nina Leeds in Eugene O'Neill's *Strange Interlude*. Certainly such feelings of guilt may contribute to her instability, but she had also been nursing for about a year and a half, first in France on the incredibly bloody western front, and then in Italy. As we now know, nurses, too, can suffer battle fatigue, particularly when the losses they see daily are compounded by close, personal ones. In addition, Catherine is in a strange country where she does not speak the language and is cloistered: "'The Italians didn't want women so near the front. So we're all on very special behavior. We don't go out.'" She and Ferguson are two British nurses serving in Italy. Through Hemingway's selection of detail, we see no British males at the British hospital in Gorizia, although British ambulance units are mentioned, and few English-speaking males at all at the American hospital in Milan: Besides Frederic, there are three other patients and Mr. Meyers (whether vice-consul McAdams and the opera singers Simmons and Saunders ever visit is never specified). If she wishes to start her social life over with a male who speaks her own language, her choices are limited, as Hemingway said of himself and his [real-life] romance with Agnes von Kurowsky: "I know now that the paucity of Americans doubtless had a great deal to do with it." Frederic Henry may not be much, but he doesn't have any competition, especially since Catherine makes her commitment to him in Gorizia at their second meeting:

> I kissed her hard and held her tight and tried to open her lips; they were closed tight. I was still angry and as I held her suddenly she shivered. I held her close against me and could feel her heart beating and her lips opened and her head went back against my hand and then she was crying on my shoulder.
>
> "Oh, darling," she said. "You will be good to me, won't you?"
>
> What the hell, I thought. I stroked her hair and patted her shoulder. She was crying.
>
> "You will, won't you?" She looked up at me. "Because we're going to have a strange life."

Frederic is obviously still on the make, but just as apparent is Catherine's surrender to the situation and commitment to a long-term relationship, apparent in her last comment. As Fetterley says, anticipating Wexler, "It is Catherine who creates the involvement between herself and Frederic."

Catherine's Commitment

Initially, Catherine's surrender is an act of will, not one of romance. It is a commitment, in several senses. As Ken Kesey later did in *One Flew Over the Cuckoo's Nest*, also punning on McMurphy's commitment to both the mental hospital and the welfare of his fellow inmates, so Hemingway has Catherine commit herself, not just to a man, but once more to life and love and the possibilities of new pain involved. In that regard, she is like all of his heroes who attempt to achieve something regardless of the odds.... And like all romantic relationships that last till the death of one of the couple, this one survives through effort, at first, all Catherine's. She nurses Frederic; she, again in two senses of the word, cares for him. She bathes him, feeds him, gives him an enema, takes him on outings and makes love to him. Except for the last item, the list might be those things a mother does for a child. As Bell says, "in the isolation of his hospital bed . . . like a baby in a bassinet, he is totally passive, tended and comforted by female caretakers. . . . The ministering of Catherine, who looks after all his needs, including sexual, . . . is more maternal than connubial."

As both Reynolds and [Scott] Donaldson note, Frederic at first is the passive accepter of services, Catherine the donor. Carlos Baker said of her that "she half-mothers, half-mistresses Frederick [sic] Henry. . . . Where she is, home is." In her maternal way, she does endow each site they occupy with a sense of home and security: the hospital room in Milan, the rented room in Montreux, even the red plush hotel room in Milan. It is unusual for a patient, even one of months' duration, to refer to his place of treatment as a home, but so Frederic repeatedly does. On a wider scale, it should be noted that it is Catherine who picks both Montreux and Lausanne as their homes in Switzerland. But her efficacy is not limited only to traditional feminine roles.

A ROLE REVERSAL

As Robert Lewis noted, "Catherine, who orders some drinks, has assumed the active, male role," and Hemingway indicates her authority in several subtle ways and just as deftly undercuts Frederic's. First, Frederic is portrayed as something considerably less than brave, mature, and thoroughly macho:

> It made me feel very young to have the dark come after dusk and then remain. It was like being put to bed after supper.
>
> I had the feeling of a boy who thinks of what is happening at a certain hour at the schoolhouse from which he has played truant.
>
> The war seemed as far away as the football games of some one else's college.

Before his operation, Frederic asks Catherine to be on duty that night so that they may again make love, not realizing the seriousness of the surgery or of his postoperative state. Nor is he aware of the danger in enlisting in the Italian army just because he happens to be in Rome when Italy enters the war in 1915. He also insists that he will not talk under the anesthetic. Catherine replies: "Now you're bragging, darling. You know you don't need to brag. . . . you sleep like a little boy with your arm around the pillow." She corrects him similarly later when he drinks a water glass one-third full of cognac: "That was very big. . . . I know brandy is for heroes. But you shouldn't exaggerate."

Also, he is jealous of her dead fiancé and insecure, and when Ferguson makes a scene at Stresa, Frederic is too naive to recognize her envy:

[Frederic:] "I don't think she wants what we have."
[Catherine:] "You don't know much, darling, for such a wise boy."

Nor is Henry exceptionally competent as a soldier. He is chagrined to learn after his return from leave that "it evidently made no difference whether I was there to look after things or not," as well as being aware that he does not deserve the silver medal awarded him by the Italian government:

[Rinaldi:] "Did you do any heroic act?"
[Frederic:] "No. . . . I was blown up while we were eating cheese."

And while one cannot easily see any alternative he might have attempted, he does not carry out his orders to evacuate the vehicles he commands, as he himself acknowledges: "all I had to do was to get to Pordenone with three ambulances. I had failed at that."

In contrast to these examples of immaturity or ineptness on Frederic's part, Hemingway indicates Catherine's maturity and leadership. When the lovers separate in Milan, Frederic stands in the street in the pouring rain, while Catherine, in the carriage, "pointed in toward the archway." Frederic finally has the intelligence to realize that "she meant for me to get in out of the rain." When they first meet, Catherine is carrying "a thin rattan stick like a toy riding-crop, bound in leather. . . . 'It belonged to a boy who was killed last year. . . . They sent me the little stick. His mother sent it to me. They returned it with his things.'" The stick's origin is the object carried by one of the models for Catherine, Elsie Jessup, who also lost a fiancé in France. Bernice Kert describes it as a walking stick; I think Carlos Baker is more correct in calling it a swagger stick.

The English did employ cavalry at the Battle of the Somme in 1916, where Catherine's fiancé was "blown up," but Hemingway describes the object "like a toy riding-crop," not very serviceable in battle; moreover, why would the boy's mother consider a riding crop a suitable memento? A swagger stick is more likely, given both Hemingway's description of it and the habits of British officers. A swagger stick is a miniature scepter, a symbol of authority; it is also a strange gift from a mother-in-law to be, unless perhaps she wished to demonstrate—swagger stick or riding crop—that Catherine had the upper hand, the whip hand, in the relationship with her son, as she also does with Frederic Henry.

TEACHING THE LESSON OF LOVE

As Reynolds and [Bernard] Oldsey have informed us, among the titles Hemingway considered for *A Farewell to Arms* were several based on [French novelist Gustave] Flaubert's *L' Education sentimentale*: "Education of the Flesh," "The Carnal Education," "The Sentimental Education of Frederick [sic] Henry," and "The Sentimental Education." If the priest had added "to feel for others," along with "serve" and "sacrifice," then we could see how successful Catherine has been. She does cause Frederic to sacrifice for others, to serve others, and to feel for others. Benson, Reynolds, and Donaldson have all painted Frederic as the less admirable of the two, more passive, the acceptor of services, and less decent. As Reynolds says, "He [Henry] has done little that was heroic, nothing admirable or particularly virtuous. . . . Surviving is the only virtue permitted him." "If the reader accepts Catherine as the heroine of the novel, it is because Frederic is always aware of her sacrifice and her death." "By the end of the novel, it is Catherine who dominates the action; Frederic has been reduced in stature while Catherine has gained."

I don't want to emphasize here the cruelty of the world as it kills the good and separates lovers. I do want to emphasize the role of Catherine Barkley as ministrant, mentor, and teacher. She maturely decides to make a commitment, to love someone who she knows does not love her, and to take full responsibility for her actions throughout, including the pregnancy that occurs. In the dance of their relationship, Catherine leads, and leads so subtly that Frederic never perceives her guidance as more than concern for him. By her example and devotion, she does cause Frederic Henry to fall in love with her. He tells her, "Now if you aren't with me I haven't a thing in the world." In Earl Rovit's terms, Catherine is the tutor, Frederic the tyro [a novice]; thus she is the Hemingway hero, defining her own course of life insofar as is possible, and teaching others—and here, the lesson is love.

Frederic Henry: A Selfish Lover

Scott Donaldson

Many critics feel that Frederic Henry and Catherine Barkley are a perfect romantic couple, but Scott Donaldson finds their relationship much more problematical. Catherine, having lost a previous lover she could not give herself to completely, seeks to lose herself in Frederic—to love, not wisely, but too well. Frederic, on the other hand, remains selfish despite his love for Catherine, and never comes close to the self-sacrificing devotion that his friend the priest characterizes as true love. Donaldson further argues that in showing Frederic's shortcomings, Hemingway distances himself from his main character. Scott Donaldson has taught at the College of William and Mary. He is the author of books on F. Scott Fitzgerald, John Cheever, and Hemingway.

A Farewell to Arms has usually been interpreted as a tragic tale of two lovers, driven together by the war, who selflessly give themselves to each other in an affair that might have lasted in indefinite bliss had not fateful death unjustly intervened to snatch one away. The events of the novel, one critic remarks, take on a "fully idyllic" cast as Frederic Henry recalls them. Frederic and Catherine Barkley, according to another, represent counterparts "of Paolo and Francesca, of Lucy and Richard Feverel, of all great lovers," with only Hemingway's realistic presentation keeping them from "heroic scale." But to read *A Farewell to Arms* in this way drastically minimizes Hemingway's accomplishment. The construction of his 1929 book is far subtler and more complicated than that of the conventional sentimental novel, and the story it has to tell is anything but straight forward.

Hemingway himself provided an important clue to his novel when he remarked to a group of University of Hawaii professors

Excerpted from Scott Donaldson, *By Force of Will: The Life and Art of Ernest Hemingway* (New York: Viking.). Copyright © Scott Donaldson, 1977. Reprinted by permission of the author.

in 1941 that their students should not be reading *A Farewell to Arms*, since it was "an immoral book." Let them read [his first novel] *The Sun Also Rises* instead, he suggested; that was "very moral." In the earlier novel, Hemingway felt he had demonstrated the evils of wasting one's resources on dissipation and sex. The message of *The Sun Also Rises*, he assured dozens of correspondents, was that "promiscuity" didn't pay. In calling *A Farewell to Arms* immoral by comparison, Hemingway was applying the same ethical standards, and lamenting that he had not made clearer Frederic Henry's own complicity in the corruption that surrounds him.

Though Lieutenant Henry encounters in Europe a world he never made, he succumbs with suspicious ease to the temptations which the war's climate of moral ambiguity presents to him. Like the sodden expatriates of Paris and Pamplona [in *The Sun Also Rises*], he regularly drinks to excess, and when in his cups blasphemes and whores like a trooper. Having acquired Catherine as a replacement for the whores, he impregnates her and then returns to the front, where during the retreat he loses his ambulances, shoots one Italian soldier in cold blood, and leads another to his death before deserting to save his own life. Then he escapes to Switzerland with his girl, who later dies bearing his child, but to whom, until she lies dying in a Lausanne hospital, he gives very little of himself.

In short, the character Frederic Henry, whom Rinaldi calls "the remorse boy," has a great deal to be remorseful about. In dealing with his own sins, moreover, he tries to smooth them away, just as he had tried to brush the taste of harlotry away with toothpaste. The entire novel may reasonably be construed as his attempt to excuse himself from blame. But Hemingway does not let his storyteller off so easily. He makes it clear, between the lines, that we should take what Lieutenant Henry has to say with a grain of salt. The difficulty in grasping this point derives from the reader's tendency to identify with Frederic, who as first-person narrator serves as guide to what happens in the novel. He seems a trustworthy enough guide to the *action*. But as Hemingway warned, even when he wrote a novel in the first person, he could not be held responsible "for the *opinions* of the narrator."

FREDERIC THE BOY

People are always misspelling Frederic Henry's name, and no wonder: only once in the book does Hemingway supply it, in full, and those who know him best usually do not call him by any name at all. What is significant is what they do call him. Only during their last meeting, for example, does his great friend and roommate Rinaldi address him by name as "Federico" and "Fred." These nicknames (like the "Rinin" Frederic uses for Rinaldi) suggest how close these two "war brothers" are, but are not nearly as suggestive as the term of affection which Rinaldi consistently and repeatedly uses in talking to Frederic. That term is "baby."

In conversation together, Frederic naturally refers to the priest as "father," but the priest does not call him "son" in return. Instead, during an early encounter (a scene which does not actually take place in the book), the priest had called Frederic "a boy." This we discover when Catherine, who is mad "only a little sometimes," directs Frederic Henry through a charade designed to let her pretend that he is a reincarnation of the fiancé she lost in the "ghastly show" at the Somme. Do this, do that, touch me so, she tells him: Frederic follows directions, and she observes, in approval, that he is "a very good boy." That, he replies, is what the priest had said.

In the light of this curious scene, where Frederic is instructed to call her "Catherine" and to say "I've come back to Catherine in the night," it is the more remarkable that nowhere in the novel does Catherine Barkley refer to her lover by name. Her most frequent endearment for him is "darling," but on several occasions she too reverts to the use of "boy." Sending him off to the front, she cautions him, as one would a child, to "be a good boy" and "be careful." When he wants to make love again before his operation in Milan, she calls him "such a silly boy"; when he sleeps with his arm around the pillow, he reminds her of "a little boy." Nor are Catherine and the priest the only ones to see Frederic Henry as a boy. The first nurse at Milan calls him "a sick boy," and Frederic objects not to the noun but the adjective: "I'm not sick. I'm wounded." The house doctor cautions him to be "a good boy" until Dr. Valentini can come. Valentini arrives and cheerfully tells him he is "a fine boy." Rinaldi understands that Frederic must regard himself as "the fine good Anglo-Saxon boy." "Poor baby," he says when Frederic admits to being in love; "poor boy," Count Greffi remarks when Frederic admits to being in religious doubt.

Whether they use "baby" or "boy," then, the other characters in *A Farewell to Arms* clearly perceive Frederic Henry as young, inexperienced, and unaware. The officers in the mess conduct their priest-baiting ritual primarily for his dubious benefit as greenhorn, and in the same fraternity-initiation spirit his fellow officers involve him in drinking contests and propel him in the direction of the bawdy house. But the sense in which Frederic Henry most clearly qualifies for boyhood rather than manhood is illustrated at Stresa, after he and Catherine have been reunited. Appearing unexpectedly, Frederic breaks up the vacation trip of Catherine and her friend Ferguson, who is bitter about that and angry at Frederic for getting Catherine with child. "Be nice to her" anyway, Catherine tells him later, for "we have so much" and Ferguson has so little. "I don't think she wants what we have," Frederic says, which moves Cat to observe: "You don't know very much, darling, for such a wise boy."

Indeed he does not, and his inability to put himself in Ferguson's place is typical of a strain of selfishness characteristic of the young. A mere boy, Frederic Henry suffers at the beginning of the novel from a pervasive lack of awareness. He does not know why he has enlisted in the Italian army, nor what he is fighting for. He lacks any perceptible ambition or purpose in life beyond the securing of his own pleasure. During the course of his war experiences he does to some degree grow in understanding. Anyone exposed to such a series of shocks—the unreasonable wound, the bollixed-up retreat, the death of his lover—might be expected to acquire from them not only trauma but, as Hemingway himself put it, "a certain working knowledge." The question at issue involves the extent of his education, how far Frederic Henry moved along the continuum from ignorant, self-centered youth to knowing, caring adulthood.

Two Kinds of Love

The contrast between sacred and profane love is established in the very first scene of *A Farewell to Arms*. Frederic is drinking the afternoon away with a friend in the Villa Rossa, the officers' whorehouse, when the priest walks by. "My friend . . . pounded on the window to attract his attention. The priest looked up. He saw us and smiled. My friend motioned for him to come in. The priest shook his head and went on." Later the priest provides his definition of love, which has nothing to do with the passion and lust of the nights Frederic has told him about. "When you love," the priest—with Hemingway—insists, "you wish to do things for. You wish to sacrifice for. You wish to serve."

Henry learns from the priest that love is more than sex, that—as Count Greffi later assures him—being in love "is a religious feeling" as well, that true lovers wish to serve and to sacrifice. But actually living up to this gospel of sacred love is very difficult. Neither Catherine nor Frederic, in fact, manages to achieve the state of ideal, selfless love which the priest describes, though they fail for strikingly different reasons.

This difference is important, because it is one of the ways in which Hemingway distances himself from his narrator. Their love, as Frederic re-creates it, was supposedly shared equally; yet Catherine is far more devoted to Frederic than he to her. Her devotion goes so far beyond proper bounds as to amount, in the end, to nothing less than heresy. When they first meet, Catherine is an emotional wreck because she had not given herself to the fiancé who had been blown up at the Somme, and she sets out to correct that error with Frederic. She throws herself—all of herself—into the affair. She arranges to be transferred to Frederic's hospital in Milan, and on arrival immediately climbs into his bed, a practice she continues repeatedly thereafter at some risk to her position as a nurse and with the eventual result of pregnancy. She willingly accompanies her lover up Lake Maggiore in a rowboat during a rainstorm on a dark night, never complains of the discomforts of being pregnant except to worry that Frederic may be bored, and even when dying thinks principally of him: "Poor darling" and "Don't worry, darling."

CATHERINE'S LOVING "TOO WELL"

Her single goal is to serve and protect Frederic Henry. Sexually, Catherine wants to please him more than the whores he has known, and she can do so, for unlike them she has no ulterior motives: "I want what you want.... Just what you want." She comforts him after his desertion, and provides a world of physical sensation which keeps him, at least temporarily, from thinking about the war. She makes a tent of her hair for them to hide inside of, pulls his cape around to cover them both. "I can keep you safe," she says. "I know I can." Discovering that he might be arrested, she proposes that they leave Italy at once: "I'll get you some place where they can't arrest you," she tells him, "and then we'll have a lovely time."

Catherine's eagerness to serve and sacrifice for Frederic apparently stems from a powerful drive to obliterate herself. On several occasions, she insists that she has submerged her personality into Frederic's. "There isn't any me any more," she remarks after they make love. And again, "there isn't any me. I'm you. Don't make up a separate me." Then, on their last night together in Milan, she implies that a two-way merger has now been completed: "We really are the same one...." During all these assertions, Frederic keeps his own counsel. Only once, near the end of the novel, does he repeat her theory about their unity, and then he does so, paradoxically, in order to keep her from trying to be more like him. Now large with child, Catherine proposes that he let his hair grow and that she cut hers and then "we'd be just alike only one of us blonde and one of us dark." But Frederic thinks his hair is long enough now, and adds, "I wouldn't let you cut yours." When she persists, he invokes the phrase which he hopes will reassure her:

"Wouldn't you like it short?" [Catherine asks.]
"I might. I like it the way it is."
"It might be nice short. Then we'd both be alike. Oh, darling, I want you so much I want to be you too."
"You are. We're the same one."
"I know. At night we are."
"The nights are grand."

Whatever Frederic may say, he is clearly not interested in losing himself in her or any unit they may form together. Nor are they "the same one," even at night, as Hemingway reveals in the scene immediately following. The lovers are both awake in the middle of the night, and Catherine starts a chat which Frederic abruptly terminates by suggesting that she should go to sleep. Catherine agrees, but adds: "Let's go to sleep at the same moment." "All right," Frederic replies, but she goes back to sleep promptly and he lies awake alone "for quite a long time." In her worshipful attitude toward Frederic, the best Catherine can hope for is that she might look like him, by cutting her hair, or act like him, by going to sleep at the same time. When the doctors sew her up after the Caesarean, the scene in the operating room looks "like a drawing of the Inquisition," and justly so, for she has committed the unpardonable sin of heresy. "You're my religion," she tells Frederic, and she means it.

FREDERIC'S LESSER LOVE

If Catherine fails to meet the priest's ideal formulation by loving not wisely but too well, with the prudential Frederic the case is quite the opposite. As the book progresses, he becomes more loving and less selfish, but only as compared to an initial policy toward Catherine that can best be defined as exploitative. During their first meetings in Gorizia, Catherine poignantly reveals her vulnerability, but Frederic nonetheless treats her as he would any other potential conquest—as an opponent in the game of seduction he intends to win. He goes through the preliminary steps, saying "I love you" when he "did not love Catherine Barkley nor had any idea of loving her." In Milan he has his reward for playing the game well, except that when she turns up at the hospital, he finds himself suddenly "crazy in love with her" though "God knows . . . he had not wanted to fall in love with any one."

The love he feels is almost entirely sexual, however, and derives from the pleasure she gives him, pleasure far superior to that dispensed by the girls at the Villa Rossa who "climbed all over you and put your cap on backward as a sign of affection between their trips upstairs with brother officers." Since he is bedridden, she must come to him, a practice which symbolizes his role, then and later, as an accepter, not a giver, of services.

During the winter of 1918, according to Frederic's retrospective reminiscences, their love reaches its most idyllic stage. Waiting for Catherine's baby to come, they live in the mountains above Montreux, alone except for the landlord and his wife (who were "very happy together too"), and as Frederic remembers it, "We had a fine life. We lived through the months of January and February and the winter was very fine and we were very happy." The flatness of the prose and the ominous touch about having "lived through" two winter months tend to undercut the explicit statement, but even more contradictory is the novel's revelation of how they spent their time.

Happiness for Catherine consists of the opportunity to be alone, for the most extended period possible, with the man she worships. When they go to the racetrack in Milan with Mr. and Mrs. Meyers and others, she finds the company insupportable: "But, darling, I can't stand so many people." "We don't see many," he objects, but she leads him off anyway to watch the next race and have a drink alone. On this occasion she senses a certain reluctance in Frederic. Didn't he like it better when they were alone? Didn't being with the others make him feel lonely? He agrees but with monosyllabic curtness, and she capitulates, "Don't let me spoil your fun, darling. I'll go back whenever you want."

While recovering from his wounds in Milan, Frederic hardly lacks for fellowship—the doctors, the nurses, Simmons, Saunders, Ettore, the American vice-consul, the head waiter at the Gran Italia—or for activity, once he is ambulatory and can go to the Ospedale Maggiore for his therapy treatments, to San Siro for the races, to the Anglo-American Club. In Switzerland, by way of contrast, he and Catherine know no one at all. For her, the Guttingens' cottage above Montreux represents the perfect location, since they can cut off all ties there. Earlier, when they'd considered where to spend his leave, she had expressed no preference: "Anywhere," as she put it, where "we don't know people." At Stresa, she had been resentful of the brief time Frederic spent in the billiard room with Count Greffi. But Frederic has no old friends or companions in Switzerland. "Isn't it grand how we never see any one?" she asks him. "You don't want to see people, do you, darling?" Frederic dutifully answers, "No," but there is evidence that he finds the exclusive pleasure of her company somewhat oppressive.

There is not much for the lovers to do in the mountains. They eat. They sleep. They read books and magazines bought in the town below. They buy a copy of "Hoyle" and play two-handed card games. They play chess. At the beginning Frederic had compared his sexual pursuit of Catherine to a chess game; now he prefers the game itself to making love:

[Frederic]: "Now do you want to play chess?"
[Catherine]: "I'd rather play with you."
"No. Let's play chess."
"And afterward we'll play?"
"Yes."
"All right."

In short, they kill time, since her job had ended with her pregnancy and his with his desertion.

In the way of "the winter sport," he and Catherine take walks together, but neither of them knows how to ski. The doctor says she can't risk it, but Frederic eagerly asserts to

Mr. Guttingen's proposal that he learn how from their son. Sensitive to his moods, Catherine detects Frederic's restlessness and halfheartedly asks whether he'd like "to go on a trip somewhere by yourself . . . and be with men and ski." Because he knows she would be devastated if he did leave, he refuses the suggestion. As an alternative, she proposes that he grow a beard:

> "All right. I'll grow one. I'll start now this minute. It will give me something to do."
> "Are you worried because you haven't anything to do?"
> "No. I like it. I have a fine life. Don't you?"

But growing a beard does not really amount to "something to do," and two pages later, while he once more reassures her that he will stay with her, Frederic reverses himself about having "a fine life." "I won't ever go away," he promises. "I'm no good when you're not there. I haven't any life at all any more." The difference between them is clearcut here. Catherine has no life without him, and desires none. Frederic has no life at all, and yearns for the occupation and companions he has left behind.

Short of idolizing her, Frederic could hardly have equaled the intensity of Catherine's love for him. But had he been more careful not to hurt her feelings, he would not have said that growing a beard would (at least) "give him something to do" or that he hadn't "any life at all any more." This latter gaffe repeats one he had made at Stresa, when he told her with exquisite lack of consideration that "My life used to be full of everything. Now if you aren't with me I haven't a thing in the world." But it is not her fault that, like "Othello with his occupation gone," he has left behind with Shakespeare's great warrior—the implied comparison belittles Frederic's relative lack of bravery and military accomplishment—the "pride, pomp and circumstance of glorious war!"

The most striking example of Frederic's insensitivity, however, comes in the scene where Catherine tells him she is pregnant. She brings up the subject reluctantly, afraid that the revelation will "worry" him or make him unhappy. She apologizes for her condition ("I took everything but it didn't make any difference"), offers him a drink to stop his worrying and make him more cheerful, promises that she will see to all the details of finding a place for the baby to be born, but Frederic merely lies in bed, does not reassure her or touch her. Finally she takes his hand, and this dialogue follows:

"You aren't angry are you, darling?"

"No."

"And you don't feel trapped."

"Maybe a little. But not by you."

"I didn't mean by me. You mustn't be stupid. I meant trapped at all."

"You always feel trapped biologically."

She went away a long way without stirring or removing her hand.

"'Always' isn't a pretty word."

It certainly isn't, implying as it does that Frederic has had his share of affairs and gotten any number of girls pregnant, and they've always made him feel trapped when they got that way. "But you see," Catherine points out, "I've never had a baby and I've never even loved any one. And I've tried to be the way you wanted and then you talk about 'always.'"

He could, Frederic says, cut off his tongue, but he goes on to pick a quarrel with her as to whether or not she's "an authority" on the question of bravery and sends her away without the psychological comfort of love-making. She will visit him later in the night, but for the moment he prefers reading the old Boston papers with their stale news to making love.

Another instance of Frederic's callousness follows shortly thereafter, when on their last night together in Milan, having worked out the details in advance, he takes her to a hotel of assignation where no luggage is required, where the normal practice is to pay in advance, where the rooms are furnished in red plush with many mirrors, and where Catherine is made to feel, inevitably and unavoidably, like a whore.

Throughout their affair, Frederic rarely displays honest and thoughtful concern for Catherine's feelings. Where she invariably thinks of him first, he often does not think of her at all. Only when she lies dying of childbirth in the Lausanne hospital does he finally begin to want to serve and to sacrifice for her. As her pain intensifies, the doctor lets Frederic administer the anesthetic, and though he is afraid of the "numbers above two," he is also glad of the chance to be of help: "It was very good of the doctor to let me do something." Then her fatal hemorrhaging starts, and he asks, pleadingly, "Do you want me to do anything, Cat? Can I get you anything?" But there is nothing to be done, and in frustration he rails at the universe.

The creator of Frederic Henry believed in retribution, in rewards and punishments, in actions producing consequences. In correspondence, Hemingway scornfully condemned those who behaved badly and then "gaily" informed the world that it was not their fault at all. But this is precisely the procedure that Frederic follows near the end of *A Farewell to Arms*. In an attempt to justify himself, he fixes all blame on a deterministic world. "The world" stands against the lovers; a vague "they" are at fault: "Now Catherine would die. That was what you did. You died. You did not know what it was about. You never had time to learn. They threw you in and told you the rules and the first time they caught you off base they killed you." Adopting the rhetorician's device of the second person "you," Frederic tries to gain his audience's assent to this philosophy. But there is a logical inconsistency in the terrible game of life-and-death he posits: though he is at least an equal partner in any mistakes that have been made, he survives and Catherine dies.

Symbolic Dogs and Ants

This philosophy rings false, furthermore, in the light of two incidents which Hemingway includes in the final chapter. In each, Frederic has the opportunity to alter the course of events for the better; in each, he responds by doing nothing constructive, instead retreating into a passivity which enables him to see himself as a person things happen *to*, rather than one who makes them happen. The first incident involves a scavenging dog Frederic discovers nosing at a refuse can early on the morning of the day Catherine dies. "What do you want?" he asks the dog and looks in the can, but "there was nothing on top but coffee grounds, dust and some dead flowers." Frederic says, "There isn't anything, dog," to underline the symbolic nihilism [the belief that life is meaningless] of the scene—but his efforts to help the dog find food have been halfhearted at best, since he has not looked beneath the surface layer.

The other incident takes the form of Frederic's reflection on a naturalistic death scene in his past:

> Once in camp I put a log on top of the fire and it was full of ants. As it commenced to burn, the ants swarmed out and went first toward the centre where the fire was; then turned back and ran toward the end. When there were enough on the end they fell off into the fire. Some got out, their bodies burnt and flattened, and went off not knowing where they

were going. But most of them went toward the fire and then back toward the end and swarmed on the cool end and finally fell into the fire. I remember thinking at the time that it was the end of the world and a splendid chance to be a messiah and lift the log off the fire and throw it out where the ants could get off onto the ground. But I did not do anything but throw a tin cup of water on the log, so that I would have the cup empty to put whiskey in before I added water to it. I think the cup of water on the burning log only steamed the ants.

In this passage, the narrator crucially, if unconsciously, condemns himself while simultaneously making nonsense of the deterministic world picture he has been advocating. Here no omnipotent fate decrees the death of the ants. They die because a camper, who might have saved them, steams them instead while clearing his cup for a drink of whisky, since he knows that water should be added to whisky and not the other way around.

UNEASY ABOUT FREDERIC HENRY

A number of readers have confessed to a certain uneasiness about Frederic Henry, among them Holden Caulfield, the young rationalizer of J.D. Salinger's *Catcher in the Rye*, who senses a certain "insincerity" in Hemingway's narrator. As [critic] E.M. Halliday observed, the philosophical reflections in the novel seem to be tacked on: "One is likely to feel not so much that Frederic Henry thought these thoughts at the time, as that Frederic Henry—or Ernest Hemingway—thought them retrospectively, and is delivering short lectures with his eyes on the audience rather than on the story itself." But it is not *either* Frederic Henry *or* Ernest Hemingway but only the created character who attempts under cover of the doctrine of determinism to evade responsibility years after the fact of his affair with Catherine Barkley. Worse yet, he does not love Catherine as she deserves. He takes without giving. He withholds. By showing us these shortcomings in Frederic Henry and by implicitly repudiating his philosophical justifications, Hemingway distances himself from his protagonist, who is one of those first-person narrators whose opinions are not to be trusted.

Excerpt from *A Reader's Guide to Ernest Hemingway*: A Farewell to Arms

Arthur Waldhorn

As is the case with many of Hemingway's young heroes, Frederic Henry is tutored in the ways of life by other characters in the novel. The surgeon Rinaldi and the young priest represent polar opposites between which Frederic must make his way, caught between the pleasure-seeking philosophy of the surgeon and the selflessness preached by the holy man. Frederic's interactions with these character foils form an important part of the education of a young man. Arthur Waldhorn has taught at the City College of New York. In addition to two books on Hemingway, he has published *Word Mastery Made Simple*, *English Made Simple*, and *Good Reading: A Guide for Serious Readers*.

Like most apprentices in Hemingway's fiction, Frederic Henry absorbs what others teach, then acts at last on his own resolve. His situation is again different, however, for he has no wholly exemplary male figure before him, no one like Pedro Romero who has "the greatness." Besides, at the outset, Frederic's self-image is so atrophied as to prohibit any exercise of will. He has, in fact, drifted into his role, apparently unaware of motive or purpose. At least he offers no explanation of why he has abandoned his studies in architecture, or even—barring a vague notion about defeat—why he has volunteered to serve in the Italian ambulance corps. About family, he refers casually to a letter from his grandfather "containing family news, patriotic encouragement, a draft for two hundred dollars, and a few clip-

---

Excerpt from "*A Farewell to Arms*," in *A Reader's Guide to Ernest Hemingway*, by Arthur Waldhorn. Copyright © 1972 by Arthur Waldhorn. Reprinted by permission of Farrar, Straus & Giroux.

pings" [141], and cynically to a stepfather whom Catherine need never meet. When first observed among others, he is sitting with his friend Rinaldi at the window of the officers' whorehouse drinking and staring at the snow outside. That evening at mess, he is conspicuously silent as his comrades debate whether he should spend his leave amid the fleshpots of the big cities or, as the priest urges, in the clear, dry countryside of Abruzzi.

Frederic's intention, he tries weeks later to explain to the disappointed priest, had been to take his holiday at the priest's home in the Abruzzi, "where the roads were frozen and hard as iron, where it was clear cold and dry..." [13]. Yet he had somehow—without wholly understanding why—yielded to the pleasures of the cities, "to the smoke of cafés... nights in bed, drunk ... and the strange excitement of waking and not knowing who it was with you... and the world all unreal in the dark... sure that this was all and all and all and not caring" [13]. Although he tries to rationalize that one never gets to do what he chooses, Henry admits to himself that the priest "had always known what I did not know and what, when I learned it, I was always able to forget. But I did not know that then, although I learned it later" [14].

This early scene is crucial to understanding the process of Frederic's "education." The long interior monologue quoted in part above defines at once his emptiness, his pained consciousness of it, and his awareness that another way of life does exist. Though he is at the outset a hollow man, knowing that he is and despairing of it mark his first step forward.[1] It is a step, however, not a stride, for Frederic still knows more than he feels about the value of life. And he cannot yet choose between the priest's way and Rinaldi's. Both of these sympathetically drawn and persuasive theorists are with him at critical moments until he is ready to act on his own during the retreat from Caporetto in Book III. Frederic's mentors are apparently polarized, the young priest an apostle of the sacred and the pure, Rinaldi of the pragmatic and the profane. Yet they share compassion and—what prevents them from becoming exemplary heroes—a need to articulate their own loneliness and desperation.

At first, Rinaldi is gay and self-assured. When he visits the wounded Frederic at the field hospital, he boasts lightly of

---

1. Rovit suggests that Frederic's emptiness is supported by a pervasive image of a "masquerade": an American disguised in an Italian uniform is how Helen Ferguson sees him; Rinaldi as an Italian in an American uniform; and to the battle police he will seem a German in an Italian uniform.

his expertise in sex and surgery, the realities that sustain him through chaos. Toward Frederic's involvement with the priest and Catherine, his mockery is mild but insistent: "You are really an Italian. All fire and smoke but nothing inside" [69]. He warns Frederic against a serious affair with Catherine, "your lovely cool goddess," pointing out that the only difference between a good girl and a woman is that with a girl the end is pain. At their next meeting, however, after Frederic returns to the front, the gentle libertine has transformed into a harsh, embittered cynic whose banter is labored, his anger genuine, his self-discipline shorn. Convinced that he has syphilis, Rinaldi is frightened, almost hysterical, arguing as "the snake of reason" against all love and in defense of the inevitability of *nada:* "You're dry and you're empty and there's nothing else . . . Not a damned thing" [180].

Much of what Rinaldi epitomizes compels Frederic's interest and sympathy, not only Rinaldi's hedonism but also his skill at his work. Yet, in his moods of despair, Rinaldi too closely resembles Frederic to teach him all he must know. True, Rinaldi's mode of life makes explicit what Frederic had not been able to explain to the priest, that the night (i.e., sensuality) is always better "unless the day was very clean and cold" (i.e., disciplined, orderly, and significant—like surgery). But as Frederic already knows and feels, Rinaldi's assumption that one learns only that all ends in disease is, however valid, too confining, especially when bounded by the precincts of a whorehouse.

The saintly young priest serves Frederic better, clarifying the choices he must at last make on his own. Unembarrassed by those who ridicule his limpid faith, the priest reminds Frederic that in his province "it is understood that a man may love God. It is not a dirty joke" [74]. To more urgent purpose, he dismisses Frederic's nights as incidents of passion and lust, not of love. "When you love you wish to do things for. You wish to sacrifice for. You wish to serve" [75]. To all this, Frederic remains ostensibly impassive, insisting that he is happy though he loves neither God nor man nor woman. Yet, when the priest leaves, Frederic lies awake for a long while thinking of the clean, orderly world that is the priest's country, a world where caring about others is natural.

At their final meeting—immediately after Rinaldi's outburst—the priest too has changed, become more subdued, less certain of his ground, less persuasive. Significantly, it is Frederic who carries the conversation now, his thoughts a curiously contradictory mixture of what he has absorbed from the priest and Rinaldi as well as from his actual experience in love and war. Early in the novel, he had argued with his drivers about their defeatism, insisting that no matter how bad or stupid war is, defeat is worse. With the priest now, Frederic momentarily shifts ground and, sounding more saintly than his companion, ventures that "it is in defeat that we become Christian . . . like our Lord . . . We are all gentler now because we are beaten" [184]. A moment later he retracts, saying that he cannot believe in defeat, even if it is better. When the priest presses him about what he does believe in, Frederic evades the query with a quip, responding––as Rinaldi might have—"In sleep." Out of such a paralysis of psychic resolve, Frederic must discover a means to move toward choice.

Dramatically effective and entirely credible, Frederic's exchanges with Rinaldi and the priest constitute an important part of his early education in the theory of life.

Frederic's and Catherine's Role Reversal

Michael S. Reynolds

In this excerpt from his book *The Making of A Farewell to Arms*, Michael S. Reynolds suggests that while Frederic has the better claim to heroism at the beginning of the novel, by the end it is Catherine who emerges as the novel's true hero. Conversely, Frederic is diminished by a series of incidents in which his identity is questioned, mistaken, or taken away. Michael S. Reynolds, who has taught at North Carolina State University, has written extensively on Ernest Hemingway, and his works include three volumes of Hemingway biography: *The Young Hemingway* (1986), *Hemingway: The Paris Years* (1989), and *Hemingway: The American Homecoming* (1992).

Frederic's difficulties in the novel are several, not the least of which is his role as narrator. In telling his own story, he is self-effacing; to Catherine he characterizes himself as a mediocre baseball hitter. As a wounded soldier, he is ironically aware of how unheroic it was to be blown up while eating cheese. Frederic Henry is not a hero, and he realizes it.

Insight After the Fact

However, one must remember that Frederic is narrating the story at some remove from the action. Time has elapsed since the death of Catherine in Lausanne, and Frederic's self-effacement is in retrospect. Telling his own story, Frederic is temperamentally incapable of making himself a hero of the action. If the reader accepts Catherine as the heroine of the novel [as does critic Delbert E. Wylder], it is because Frederic is always aware of her sacrifice and her death. Frederic's insights into the nature of bravery do not, ultimately, apply to

Excerpted from Michael S. Reynolds, *Hemingway's First War: The Making of A Farewell to Arms* (Princeton, NJ: Princeton University Press, 1976). Reprinted with the permission of the author. (Footnotes in the original have been omitted in this reprint.)

his own action, but they are significant comments on Catherine Barkley:

> If people bring so much courage to this world the world has to kill them to break them, so of course it kills them. The world breaks everyone and afterward many are strong at the broken places. But those that will not break it kills. It kills the very good and the very gentle and the very brave impartially. If you are none of these you can be sure it will kill you too but there will be no special hurry.

As with all of Frederic's insights, which are embedded in the novel like polished gems, it is important to remember that this is an insight derived after the fact. More importantly, these insights are based upon the experience contained within the novel. Frederic brings no formal systems of philosophy to bear upon his experience, and because he is self-conscious of his role as narrator, his insights are not meant to enhance his own character. [Critic] Leo Gurko is mistaken in his belief that both Frederic and Catherine are meant to be the good, gentle, and brave. Frederic is incapable of seeing himself in such a light. Quite naturally he has no difficulty seeing Catherine as good, brave, and gentle, for he is alive and she is dead because of their child. One must remember that it was Frederic who early in the novel made the mistake about bravery:

> "They won't get us," I said. "Because you're too brave. Nothing ever happens to the brave."
> "They die of course." [Catherine]
> "But only once."
> "I don't know. Who said that?"
> "The coward dies a thousand deaths, the brave but one?"
> "Of course. Who said it?"
> "I don't know."
> "He was probably a coward," she said. "He knew a great deal about cowards but nothing about the brave. The brave dies perhaps two thousand deaths if he's intelligent. He simply doesn't mention them."

No matter how formally British, stiff-upper-lip Catherine may sound, she does become the brave one in the novel. Frederic, for all his skill at self-preservation, is never quite brave. He is always able to save himself; Catherine is not.

WHO FREDERIC IS NOT

Wylder is quite right, therefore, in seeing Catherine as the "hero" of the novel and in seeing Frederic as the anti-hero. However, Frederic's problem of identity goes beyond his status as hero or anti-hero, for he is identified throughout the novel in terms of negatives. The reader is constantly discovering what Frederic is *not*, or Frederic is continually being mistaken for someone he is not. When Catherine first meets him, she identifies him as *not being an Italian*. A little later when she goes a little "off," she mistakes him for her dead fiancé. When Frederic is wounded at Plava, he is mistaken for a hero. Rinaldi asks him at the field hospital:

"Did you do any heroic act?"

"No," I said. "I was blown up while we were eating cheese."

"Be serious. You must have done something heroic either before or after. Remember carefully."

"I did not."

"Didn't you carry anybody on your back? . . ."

"I didn't carry anybody. I couldn't move."

When Frederic reaches the hospital in Milan, he is mistaken for an Austrian prisoner by the Italian barber because he speaks with a foreign accent. At the bridgehead on the Tagliamento during the retreat, Frederic is first misidentified as an officer who has abandoned his troops. Then he is mistaken for an enemy infiltrator in an Italian uniform because he speaks with an accent. Once he deserts, he quickly removes the officer stars from his uniform to repudiate his former identity. He is now *not* an Italian officer, but neither is he a civilian. After he has dressed in the civilian clothes he borrows from Simmons in Milan, Frederic confesses that he feels like a masquerader. In Switzerland, he and Catherine live under false identities; first they pretend to be cousins; then they pretend to be married. During Catherine's pregnancy Frederic grows a beard in an effort to establish some form of identity. However, when he sees himself in the gym mirror as a boxer with a beard, he recognizes it as a false identity. Later in Lausanne, Frederic must put on a white doctor's gown to enter Catherine's hospital room:

> I put it on and pinned it in back at the neck. I looked in the glass and saw myself looking like a fake doctor with a beard.

In the final account the reader knows Frederic by negatives. He is not an Italian. He is not an Austrian. He is not a hero. He is not a German infiltrator. He abandons his identity as an officer, but he is not yet a civilian. He is neither Catherine's cousin nor her husband. He is not a boxer, and he is not a doctor. Such a piling-up of negative identification must finally produce a non-heroic figure.

Role Reversal

Frederic's negative identity, including a lack of a usable past, becomes ironically magnified when he and Catherine reverse roles in the novel. When the book opens it is Frederic who has the potential for heroics; his situation is more likely to produce heroic action than is Catherine's. By the end of the novel, it is Catherine who dominates the action; Frederic has been reduced in stature while Catherine has gained. This shift of focus is emphasized by the role reversal in their parallel hospital scenes: the first in Milan, the second in Lausanne.

When Frederic is first examined in the Milan hospital, he is told that his operation must wait on the natural healing process. When Catherine is first examined in the Lausanne hospital, she must wait until the natural process brings her pregnancy to termination. In both cases, however, the natural process is circumvented. Frederic insists upon an immediate operation; Catherine has no choice in the matter, for without the Caesarean she will die. In both cases there are confident doctors who have no hesitancy about the operations. Dr. Valentini operates on Frederic the morning after he first examines him; more conservative surgeons would have waited six months. In Lausanne, Catherine's doctor does not hesitate to recommend the operation: "I would advise a Caesarean operation. If it were my wife I would do a Caesarean."

Thus Frederic and Catherine are both confined to hospitals to undergo operations at the hands of confident surgeons. It is useful to note, however, that Frederic has come to the hospital via the destructive cycle of war; Catherine comes to her delivery bed as a result of the natural cycle. Moreover, her pregnancy is a direct result of the nights she spent in Frederic's hospital bed earlier.

In Milan, Catherine was the nurse and Frederic was the patient. It was Catherine who prepared Frederic for his operation, not wanting anyone else to touch him. She gave him instructions on how to behave under the gas so that he would not reveal their relationship while he was unconscious. Catherine says:

"Say your prayers then. That ought to create a splendid impression."
"Maybe I won't talk."
"That's true. Often people don't talk."

In Lausanne the roles of patient and nurse are reversed. Catherine is in the hospital bed because of her love for Frederic, and Frederic is at her bedside in the role of nurse. In Lausanne, it is Catherine who is taking gas, and it is Frederic who is concerned about the effects of the gas on the patient:

> I turned the dial to three and then four. I wished the doctor would come back. I was afraid of the numbers above two.

When wounded, Frederic showed a low tolerance for pain; in Lausanne Catherine calls her worst pains "good ones." In Milan, Catherine had worried that Frederic would expose their sexual relationship; ironically, it is Catherine who exposes them, not by her words but by her expanding womb. In Milan, Catherine had advised Frederic to say his prayers, but it is not until the hospital room in Lausanne that Frederic is able to pray. His prayers, however, do not create a "splendid impression."

Frederic, who began the novel as the active participant, has become the passive participant by the end of the novel. Whereas it was Catherine who, early in the novel, submerged her identity in Frederic; at the end of the novel it is Frederic who has lost all positive identity. He has switched roles with Catherine until he is finally left with no role to play.

CHAPTER 3
Major Themes

Frederic Henry's Heroic Rejection of Clichés

Blanche Gelfant

Despite Frederic Henry's denunciation of the clichés of war in a famous early passage, he falls back on such clichés during Catherine's crisis in childbirth late in the novel. Henry tries to reassure himself that Catherine's is an ordinary delivery and that he is just an ordinary nervous father-to-be. But Henry cannot run away from dire reality by hiding in clichés. Gelfant argues that his ability to face the situation without hiding behind clichés is a moral act that reinforces his stature as a real Hemingway hero. Blanche Gelfant has taught at Upstate Medical Center of the State University of New York at Syracuse and Dartmouth College. She is the author of *The American City Novel*, *Women Writing in America*, and *Cross-Cultural Reckonings*.

For the novelist, the danger of the cliché is not merely staleness of language; it is dullness of perception—and dullness has both esthetic and moral implications. A writer like Ernest Hemingway who held purity of language as his esthetic standard pursued clarity of vision as his moral commitment. For such a writer the relationship between the experience and the word was of utmost concern. It was a relationship that had to remain completely reciprocal: the experience was to suggest the word, and the word in turn was to recall the experience. This reciprocity is destroyed by the cliché. The cliché sets individual experiences into stereotyped patterns of perception and expression, patterns which cannot recreate accurately "the way it was" because they do not evoke the unique and modifying qualities of an experience. The cliché makes invidious use of the power of words to suggest merely other words instead of actualities.

From Blanche Gelfant, "Language as a Moral Code in *A Farewell to Arms*," *Modern Fiction Studies*, vol. 9, no. 2 (Summer 1963), pp. 173–76. Copyright © 1963 Purdue Research Foundation. Reprinted by permission of the Johns Hopkins University Press. (Footnotes in the original have been omitted in this reprint.)

In this way it offers an easy escape from the encounter with truth. The use of the cliché as one's idiom implies then a kind of moral capitulation, a willingness to settle for less than truth or clarity of vision and a willingness to embrace words for the comfort of their familiarity. Thus staleness of language may reflect obtuseness or evasiveness and sometimes even fear.

FREDERICK FALLS BACK ON CLICHÉS

It is fear that leads Frederick Henry in a crucial scene in *A Farewell to Arms* to fall back on the ever-ready cliché despite his earlier impassioned denunciation of its uses in war and his consistent avoidance of it in all circumstances. Frederick's brief interior monologue on the possibility of Catherine's death is interesting stylistically because Hemingway seems here to forsake the ideal of purity of expression and to rely instead upon mere banalities. The language is trite and repetitious to the point of compulsion; the sentences are distressingly simple; and the movement is erratic, syncopated by the nervous rushes and ebbs of fear. But closer study of the monologue reveals the marvelous economy of Hemingway's art as well as a highly creative use of the cliché. Through the very banalities of the passage, the repetitions, the erratic tempo and dialectic structure, Hemingway expresses simultaneously several levels of experience—Frederick's surface panic and the scurry of his immediate thoughts, the underlying depths of his anxiety, and the total moral integrity of his character.

As the monologue allows Frederick to verbalize his fears, it shows him undergoing the crucial test of the Hemingway hero. Like the young man in initiation, or the bullfighter, hunter, soldier, or prizefighter, Frederick is confronting the fact of death and so taking measure of his courage. Frederick's courage consists in the willingness to face reality. In all situations he has rejected the ready clichés with which men immure themselves in illusions, whether those of love, war, or sacrifice. For Frederick, as for most Hemingway heroes, the inescapable reality of life is death. Death is "the end of the trap." Now the trap has been sprung to catch Catherine, and Frederick, having staked his happiness on Catherine, is caught along with her. He knows that they are trapped, but he knows also that the only courageous gesture is to try to escape. Hence the passage expresses the excruciating tension of the struggle against all odds, a struggle which takes place in Frederick's mind as he returns at least ten times to the question of death in his thrashing effort to evade the inevitable. As Frederick's thoughts race back and forth from the possibility of death to denial, the movement of the passage simulates the scurrying movement of the trapped creature in a maze. Frederick's unexpressed fear that there is no way out of the maze—that death cannot be denied—leads him to the round of hackneyed but possibly reassuring expressions called forth in such moments of stress. "A bad time," "protracted initial labor," "just nature"—are these not the set phrases suitable to such an occasion?; have they not been suggested by doctor and nurse?; and should not Frederick at least try them all? Women in labor have "a bad time"; men always pace the floor. Frederick creates out of a few pat phrases a kind of incantation, as though repetition of words can exorcise the fact of death.

> She's just having a bad time. The initial labor is usually protracted. She's only having a bad time. Afterward we'd say what a bad time and Catherine would say it wasn't really so bad. But what if she should die? She can't die. Yes, but what if she should die? She can't, I tell you. Don't be a fool. It's just a bad time. It's just nature giving her hell. It's only the first labor, which is almost always protracted.

Frederick is trying to fit himself into the stereotype of "the nervous husband" so that his apprehension of death may seem nothing more than the typical cartoon-like gesture of the dishevelled, cigarette-smoking, anxious male. But as quickly as his mind touches upon generalizing stereotypes, it rejects them, for to Frederick all generalities are suspect. He has trained his mind to move from general statement to specific perception, from the word to the reality—and the reality of this situation is that no matter how typical indeed his fears may be, the possibility of Catherine's death in childbirth remains. Thus in these opening trial runs, Frederick cannot qualify his perception of the situation by clichés that cluster about "the anxious husband," just as earlier he could not conceive of war in clichés of sacrifice and glory.

THE FAILURE OF CLICHÉS

The few medical clichés he calls to mind are destined to fail, since Frederick has already seen that medical jargon often conceals sheer ignorance. He tries to fit Catherine's pain into a larger context of natural (and thus survivable) causes, but this approach leads back to another fact of nature, the indisputable fact of death. There remain the alternatives of reason and faith. What logical reason is there for Catherine to die now? Having already discounted the possibility of moral retribution for the sin of illicit love, Frederick can find no other logic for her death. But he has learned of the gratuitousness of death in war (Aymo's death, for instance, and his own near execution), and he knows that death strikes without discernible reason. Death is merely inevitable, not rational. His final response is a simple declarative assertion of faith: "She can't die." And this is the weakest position of all. So Frederick's panic increases as he is flung back again and again to the initial and still unanswered question, "But what if she should die?"

CONFRONTING BOTH LANGUAGE AND LIFE

The bewilderment and shock that Frederick feels are reflected in the helpless repetition of this question and in the accelerated pace with which it comes as his futile monologue draws to an end. He has found no way out of the trap. But by refusing to capitulate to the easy cliché and the sentimental illusion, he has maintained intellectual and moral integrity. He has done this, however, at the expense of all hope. At the conclusion of the monologue both he and the reader have the clear foreknowledge of doom. The terrible anguish inextricably bound with this knowledge is created through the "fourth dimensional" quality of Hemingway's writing, its implicatory or suggestive power; it is the anguish inherent in the frustrated and always circuitous movement of Frederick's thoughts, the pathetic meagreness of his sentences, the bare banality of his phrases, as he races frantically back and forth, trapped in a maze which has no exit. The alternative to escape, which Frederick takes, is to acknowledge the truth of the situation, and this acknowledgement is signified by the change of style, back to his clipped and precise everyday speech.

Thus Hemingway's rejection of the loose and easy formulation of the cliché, like Frederick's ultimate dismissal of it here, is in effect a refusal to capitulate to any formulation at all. The search for exactness of language becomes a moral act, implying an encounter with reality; it is the search for a code not yet defined, hence not yet expressed, and certainly not yet made meaningless by unconsidered use. When, as in this passage in *A Farewell to Arms*, Hemingway uses the cliché he makes of it a moral standard by which character is tested and revealed. And since character implies action, the cliché becomes also a device of plot to foreshadow and even to provide climactic resolution. Thus style, character, and structure reinforce each other in the novel, and perception and language become truly reciprocal.

Frederic Henry's Disillusionment with War

Jackson J. Benson

At the beginning of *A Farewell to Arms*, Frederic Henry is a "tourist through life," a man committed to a war for no real reason. According to Jackson J. Benson, his education in the novel is a process of learning about the game of love and war. After he is wounded, Henry grows progressively more realistic about the nature of war, learning the difference between the former abstract and romantic notions of fighting for a cause and a new realistic understanding of how war strips the soldier of his individuality. Only when Henry learns this lesson does he trade the game of war for that of love. Jackson J. Benson has taught at San Diego State University. He is the author of numerous books, including a highly regarded biography, *The True Adventures of John Steinbeck, Writer*.

Hemingway's ... protagonist, Frederic Henry, is a study of a man who struggles to gain awareness and finds it only when he finds a worthy commitment. An exploration into the problems of gamesmanship, *A Farewell to Arms* focuses on Lieutenant Henry's attempts to discover the full implications of two culturally defined activities, war and love, that he is only partly aware of as games. His problem, in short, is finding the right game to play. . . .

The really hellish thing about Frederic Henry is that he is a perfectly normal young man, a nice guy. This very normality is the basis for an ironic treatment that is barbed both in the direction of the young protagonist and in the direction of the reader. . . . Like many young men, Henry is rather selfish, rather casual about the suffering of others, somewhat indifferent to the consequences of his actions, willfully a vic-

From Jackson J. Benson, *Hemingway: The Writer's Art of Self-Defense*. Copyright © 1969 by the University of Minnesota. All rights reserved. Reprinted with the permission of the University of Minnesota Press. (Footnotes in the original have been omitted from this reprint.)

tim of his own self-indulgence and completely unconvinced of the possibility of his own death.

A Tourist Through Life

His main fault seems to be a general unawareness—a deadly sin within the Hemingway canon. He is, to use the Hemingway epithet applied to such people, a tourist through life and the war he has enlisted in. Frederic Henry is somewhat like a fraternity boy, a party boy, who has been motivated by an ill-defined idealism and a vague romantic urge to join the Peace Corps, only to find that he is not the star of the show. He wears his officer's uniform with a casual pride, just the right touch of nonchalance, and takes advantage of his position to attack the local contingent of nurses, as if his role required it of him. And since, fortunately, it is the Italian army that he is attached to as an ambulance officer, there is drinking and whoring even close to the front. Frederic Henry's situation at the beginning of *A Farewell to Arms* is very much like an American teen-age male's dream of overseas duty.

In his early encounters with the British nurse Catherine Barkley, Henry is the casual, uniformed boy on the make, but down deep inside he is really a decent sort. In other words, what makes Henry so sinister is his All-American-Boy lack of guile. He demonstrates an attitude and pattern of behavior that any Rotarian [member of the Rotary Club] would privately endorse. He fully intends (he spells it out quite clearly) to take a girl, who is described in terms of a helpless, trembling Henry James [the American novelist] bird, and crush her in his bands very casually as part of the game that every young, virile lad must play. It is a backhanded tribute to Hemingway's irony here that most readers don't seem to even blanch at the prospect. A further sinister element is Henry's rather bland and unexcited approach to the calculated betrayal of his neurotic young nurse—if he were drooling with lust, he would be more forgivable.

A Farewell to Arms is not a war story or a love story so much as it is a modern morality drama, the story of the developing consciousness of a young American within the characteristic twentieth-century context of war. Consciousness here has a somewhat special meaning in that the development of Henry's character is not indicated so much by changes in the quality of thinking, as it is by changes in the quality of seeing. Hemingway's technique in this novel is

>
> **ALL ARMIES ARE THE SAME**
> *The sardonic tone of this poem, which Hemingway wrote in Paris in 1922, suggests the writer's disillusionment with warfare.*
>
> All armies are the same
> Publicity is fame
> Artillery makes the same old noise
> Valor is an attribute of boys
> Old Soldiers all have tired eyes
> All Soldiers hear the same old lies
> Dead bodies always have drawn flies
>
> Ernest Hemingway, *Complete Poems*. Nicholas Gerogiannis, ed. Lincoln: University of Nebraska Press, 1979, p. 42.

very similar to that employed by many contemporary poets who use imagery rather than argument or exposition: the landscape in *A Farewell to Arms* is the landscape of Frederic Henry's mind. The problem or central term of the novel's conflict is defined very explicitly at the beginning of the novel in the words of the priest as that of "seeing." Since Henry, at the beginning of the novel, is selfish and ego-centered, his perceptions of his surroundings are vague, limited, and detached.

His youth, his egotism, his callow playacting approach to life are all indicated in his view of the war: "Well, I knew I would not be killed. Not in this war. It did not have anything to do with me. It seemed no more dangerous to me myself than war in the movies." The voice here of the older and wiser Henry looking back on his previous condition is tinged with both regret and wry prophecy—in effect, "Little did I know at the time what war was really like and how it would affect me." Although unpleasant details are brought home to the reader, the burden is not so much antiwar, as it is anti-Henry. These details are presented in such a callous, incidental way (using the same ironic understatement Hemingway had previously perfected in the *In Our Time* sketches of the war), that they reflect discredit on the observer: "At the start of the winter came the permanent rain and with the rain came the cholera. But it was checked and in the end only seven thousand died of it in the army." Particularly unpleasant in their implications regarding Henry's condition, as well as establishing the absurdity of the war itself, are those observations of the war early in the novel which bring carnage and destruction into a context reminiscent of a quaint Italian operetta: there is priest-baiting in the mess hall, a mobile house of love up the street, the Italian infantry which moves back and forth retreating from and then recapturing the same territory, and an Austrian artillery which seems to be less than serious, bombarding the town in which Henry is stationed, not "to destroy it but only a little in a military way."...

WAR AND THE LOSS OF SELF

What Henry apparently does not see is that war is a destroyer of love through its fundamental irrational violence, and war is a destroyer of the individual through its obliteration of the individual's dignity and importance. The priest calls attention to the former in trying to get Henry to see what love is as compared with the lust that accompanies war (Rinaldi calls the girls at the Villa Rossi "war comrades," they have become so familiar), and the priest calls attention to the latter by pointing to the dignity of the individual found in his home province of the Abruzzi—"it is understood that a man may love God. It is not a dirty joke." The point is that at the beginning of the novel Henry's even perfunctory commitment to the war has robbed him of both his capacity for love and his capacity to act and react as an individual—but he is unaware of this. He has not perceived that as a game war is absurd, for what rules there are have nothing to do with winning or losing, as the novel constantly points out, and are constantly contradictory and self-defeating. Until the incident at the bridge, Henry goes on trying to make war meaningful, as his attempts, within the chaos and absurdities of the retreat, to follow "orders" make clear.

War is a particularly good controlling metaphor for all those things that we have come to associate with "mass man"—the bureaucracy, the indifference, the brainwashing and propaganda, the tyranny of an overgroup devoted to the "abstract good" (and sanctified by that devotion)—in short, all those things that are accepted as normal in wartime (particularly in the modern mechanized warfare that commenced with World War I). All these are the very things that are the substance of the nightmare societies pictured, for example, in [British author George] Orwell's *1984*, in [British author Aldous] Huxley's *Brave New World*, or perhaps even more to the present point, in [Czech author Franz] Kafka's *The Castle*. It is ironic that it is so difficult for us or for Henry to perceive this effect: the worst thing about war, even more terrible than the physical suffering, because it is more subtle and insidious, is that the individual (and along with the individual, morality and responsibility) is lost and that the loss serves little purpose except to feed irrationality. All who have been in the army of any country know that the first abiding principle of service is the loss of individual volition, a literal beating down of identity, a submersion into the general, and an unquestioning submission to the impersonality of "orders."....

NOTHING IS WORSE THAN WAR

[Henry is] committed to the proposition that there is meaning somewhere in the pattern, although it may be unavailable to him. Before the attack in which the enemy shelling is to wound Henry and take him away from the front for several months, he crouches in a bunker with his ambulance drivers waiting for the time that they will be needed. The drivers talk about the coming attack. One notes that there aren't enough troops for a real attack; another suggests that "It is probably to draw attention from where the real attack will be." Do the men who are going to participate in this pretense know they are going to be bait—simply objects, pawns to be manipulated in someone else's game? "Of course they don't," another replies; "They wouldn't attack if they did." Then the drivers turn to a discussion of various troops that have refused to attack, including the story of a "big smart tall boy," who is allured by the glamour of the crack troops, the granatieri, enough to join up to show off to the girls and to associate with the carabinieri (MP's), who later shoot him for not attacking when he is ordered to. Not only is he shot, but his family is deprived of their civil rights and the protection of the law—"Anybody can take their property." At this point one of the drivers tells Henry that he should not let them talk this way. But Henry does not mind as long as they "drive the cars and behave." His attitude of commitment to the absurdity contrasts sharply with the awareness of the ambulance driver Passini in the exchange that follows.

> "I believe we should get the war over," I said. "It would not finish it if one side stopped fighting. It would only be worse if we stopped fighting."
>
> "It could not be worse," Passini said respectfully. "There is nothing worse than war."

"Defeat is worse."

"I do not believe it," Passini said still respectfully. "What is defeat? You go home."

When Henry continues to insist that being conquered is worse, Passini makes the same charge indirectly that the priest is to make later in the hospital: "There is nothing as bad as war. We in the auto-ambulance cannot even realize at all how bad it is. When people realize how bad it is they cannot do anything to stop it because they go crazy. There are some people who never realize." Many, including Catherine and later Rinaldi, "go crazy," but Lieutenant Henry is not to find this same depth of emotional realization of the war until he becomes personally involved in the absurdity of the bridge.

Henry's Wounding

The story of Lieutenant Henry's discovery begins with his being hit by fragments of a trench mortar shell. Before that, he was a "nice boy," as Catherine calls him, who argued that "defeat is worse" than war and who thought of the war as no more dangerous to himself "than war in the movies." But when he is hit, he finds that he is really in the war after all: "I tried to breathe but my breath would not come and I felt myself rush bodily out of myself and out and out and out and all the time bodily in the wind. I went out swiftly, all of myself, and I knew I was dead and that it had all been a mistake to think you just died." He is not dead, but any doubt that may remain about how close death has come to him is erased when he turns to the man next to him in the bunker. When Henry touches him, he screams and then biting his arm, the man pleads deliriously for the pain to stop, until he dies. Reaching down to examine himself, Henry puts his hand on his knee: "My knee wasn't there. My hand went in and my knee was down on my shin." The terror and shock and suffering are relentlessly conveyed by the realism of the detail. The effect on Lieutenant Henry's over-all attitude is never directly stated. It is, if stated at all, best phrased by Colonel Cantwell in another novel, *Across the River and into the Trees*, who suffered the same kind of wound under similar circumstances in the same war: "Finally he did get hit properly and for good. No one of his other wounds had ever done to him what the first big one did. I suppose it is just the loss of the immortality, he thought. Well, in a way, that is quite a lot to lose." It may be, therefore, that Lieutenant Henry has lost what Colonel Cantwell has called his "immortality." He has volunteered to serve in a war without really knowing the stakes, the price he may be called on to pay. Commitment is morally less significant without a true sense of the risk involved; one is not really putting anything on the line if he thinks he is never going to lose. Nor is he really "alive" without risking something. Like so many young men, Henry is unaware because he is wrapped up in himself—bored....

There are several ironic contrasts implicit in the story of Henry's wounding that are of some help in assessing its impact. Henry and his men are noncombatants who are waiting to perform an act of mercy in carrying the wounded to medical help. Instead of this, Henry ends up being carried in an ambulance himself, suffering the discomforts (the pain, the bumps, the slowness, and the hemorrhage of the man in the stretcher above him) of one of the men Henry would have perfunctorily transported if not himself wounded. The shells coming in from the Austrians are indiscriminate; they do not seek out the infantryman and leave the ambulance driver unharmed (just as when someone shells a city, he does not neglect the women and children and select only the soldiers or arms factories to destroy—a stupidity, as Passini would term it, which only makes sense in a pattern of stupidity). Henry is seriously wounded, not in the process of attacking, but in the process of eating. And of course, it is Passini, who so hates war, who is killed. These ironies may raise certain questions in Henry, at some level of consciousness, just as they most certainly do in the mind of the reader: What kind of game is this? Who understands the rules and the objectives that demand such a risk and such a price? Fittingly, Henry's first step to full awareness comes with the shock of physical sensation. He has become personally involved on an indisputable level of consciousness, like it or not. The next level involves a fuller realization of what war can do to others.

Henry's period of convalescence at the American hospital in Milan is primarily the story of his increasing attachment to Catherine Barkley. His connection with the war is a meager one, established through the newspapers and one or two conversations with other soldiers. At his distance from it, the war seems to take on less clarity than ever. The Italians are losing tremendous numbers of men in their offensive, and even if they go on to capture Monte San Gabriele, there are "Plenty of mountains beyond for the Austrians." He meets a British major on somebody's staff who declares that "it was all balls." At headquarters "they thought only in divisions and man-power. They all squabbled about divisions and only killed them when they got them." Again, Henry encounters the contrast of the mass with the lost individual. As an individual having been touched personally by the war, Henry is now able to stand back in an ironically impersonal perspective and get a dim glimpse of the entire meat grinder....

PLAYING THE WRONG GAME WELL

One other indicator of Henry's growing disillusionment during his stay at the hospital is the satirical treatment of Ettore, the "legitimate hero" who finds the war game very satisfying. Henry runs into Ettore and several other acquaintances at a bar while killing time away from the hospital waiting for Catherine. Ettore responds to the baiting of his companions, including Henry, who ask him all the right questions: "How many [medals] have you got, Ettore?" "How many times have you been wounded, Ettore?" "Where were you wounded, Ettore?" These are questions that probably have been asked and answered a dozen times before, as we can induce from Catherine's label of him as a bore, and from Hemingway's wonderful touch of including Ettore's name at the end of almost every question that leads him on, to provide just the right tone of mockery, a mockery unperceived by Ettore but available to the reader.

Ettore seriously recites his entire repertoire of accomplishments yet one more time with continuing and undiminished enthusiasm. He's got five medals and, Oh boy, aren't they great for making the girls think you're fine. But wound stripes are better: "Believe me, boy, when you get three you've got something"; he goes on to show his scars and describe the circumstances in detail. He points out that the real pros touch their scars, as he does, whenever anybody mentions getting killed. And when a friend, in leaving, says "Keep out of trouble," Ettore of course takes it literally and seriously announces his dedication to his profession through clean living. A further hint of irony is found in the almost perfectly complementary situation of another man in the group, an opera singer, who is so bad, despite his unbounded enthusiasm for his own singing, that everywhere he sings audiences throw things at him. Then too, Ettore provides the perfect foil to Henry's lack of engagement—overenthusiasm. Ettore has decided to play the wrong game well, and his very enthusiasm for it condemns war as ludicrous. . . .

CHANGED FRIENDS

Of much more serious impact on Lieutenant Henry's feelings toward the war are the dramatic changes he finds in his friends following the summer offensive. After he has returned to the front, he checks in with his commanding officer, the major, who now looks "older and drier." He is, as the priest comments later, now "gentle." The theme of "how bad it is" which had been taken up by Passini and the priest at the time of Henry's wounding is now taken up again upon Henry's return, this time by the major—an unexpected certification of the same sentiments previously expressed by the socialist driver and the priest. Just how bad it is comes through gradually to Henry when the major tells him that he is lucky that he got hit when he did and (an even more telling blow) when he states that "if I was away I do not believe I would come back."

More shattering still is Henry's reunion with his friend Rinaldi. Rinaldi is one of several Hemingway characters who has often been badly treated by Hemingway critics. He is usually taken at face value, accepted on the basis of what he says about himself—a dangerous practice in criticism, as in life. A hard professional, flippant and cynical, he speaks of himself (and Henry) as having "nothing inside." But as usual in Hemingway, the negative emotions are the most apparent. What we tend to see most directly is Rinaldi's cynicism about himself and his life, the anger, the depression, and the frustration that come from the overwork of a surgeon in a bloody war. Like the best bullfighters, however, Rinaldi combines his cynicism with a tremendous devoutness, a devoutness seen only obliquely. He is tough, but he is also sensitive; throughout the initial scenes with Henry, he shows a great affection for him. In what happens to Rinaldi during the summer, there is good evidence, to my mind, for the fact that here is a man who cares a great deal about people in general.

Driven beyond physical endurance by the enormous demands put on him by the offensive, he has also been driven to the wall emotionally. The picture of Rinaldi as Henry finds him on his return is not just that of a man almost shattered from exposure to the pain of others. He cannot think, for to think means to feel: "No, by God, I don't think; I operate." If he can turn himself into a mechanical man, keep busy, work all the time, perhaps he will not have time to feel. But now the offensive is over: "I don't operate now and I feel like hell. This is a terrible war, baby. You believe me when I say it." If this means that Rinaldi is simply a one-dimensional man, simply a cynical surgeon, simply a foil for Henry and his devotion to Catherine, it would not be that war is so terrible; it would not be that everything that was so funny, so full of life before the summer is now flat and dead. No man destroys himself with such vigor as Rinaldi is seen destroying himself here just because he has run out of work, unless that work has taken on more than just professional dimensions. For a surgeon such as Rinaldi, the incessant burden of life and death that the war has forced upon him has more impact than just that on his professional pride. Rinaldi's emotional destruction is the product of an emotional investment, never stated, but implicit in his behavior toward Henry and in his present wild irrationality. Neither is he a failure. He does not demonstrate to Henry the uselessness of a commitment, the failure of "the ideal of service," but rather the failure of war to allow love to exist except at a terrible price. . . .

Finding a New Game

With neither mind nor heart any longer even distantly devoted to the process of war or to victory as the lesser of two evils, it is only Lieutenant Henry's physical presence on the scene that must be accounted for. Complete withdrawal cannot be accomplished, however, until the other party to the contract, the Italian army, in some way invalidates the contract Henry is bound to whether it is meaningful to him any longer or not. There is no doubt that without the incident at the bridge or one like it, Henry would have continued to serve despite his disillusionment until the end of the war or until he was killed. We await the coup de grace.

The battle police at the bridge operate very well as symbols of the enforcement of non-meaning. They stand for everything that Henry has come to realize is false and irrational about the war. The main quality in the passage that stands out about these carabinieri is their complete, self-confident ignorance: they have no idea whatsoever of what it means to be under fire. Henry notes on two separate occasions that "the questioners had that beautiful detachment and devotion to stern justice of men dealing in death without being in any danger of it." Here, in spades, is the ultimate absurdity of commitment to the irrational that Henry has been part of. With growing awareness, however, he perceives their stubborn blindness: "They were all young men and they were saving their country." In their pursuit of the cliché, they shoot everyone they question, for the questions are not really requests for information, but the recitation of the litany of war.

The absurdity of the game that Henry has pledged himself to is revealed in the contrast brought out here between the rules, rituals, rhetoric, and values of the pretense, and the reality which at its worst can involve panic, cowardice, brutality, suffering, destruction, and death. All the human elements, the pity and the terror of the *individual*, are lost on these minds which find war glorious and filled with purpose. The basis of game, as we have defined it, is its framework of rationality; the very basis of war as seen here is its irrationality. While the Austrians and Germans roam the countryside unopposed, the Italians have applied the most immediate practical solution: they have decided to shoot all of their own officers.

These elements of reality and unreality are nowhere better contrasted than in the interview (observed by Henry) between the battle police and the "fat gray-haired little lieutenant-colonel" who is taken out of the retreating column for "questioning":

"It is you and such as you that have let the barbarians onto the sacred soil of the fatherland," [said the battle police].

"I beg your pardon," said the lieutenant-colonel.

"It is because of treachery such as yours that we have lost the fruits of victory."

"Have you ever been in a retreat?" the lieutenant-colonel asked.

"Italy should never retreat." . . .

"If you are going to shoot me," the lieutenant-colonel said, "please shoot me at once without further questioning. The questioning is stupid."

Reason is lost. This is the country of the slogan. Unlike Henry, the colonel has no choice except to try to give his death what dignity he can. Not only is a human life destroyed for no good reason, but a valuable professional has been stupidly thrown away. For Henry, younger and more objective in his position, an alternative to a stupid death does present itself, and he takes it, dashing down to the water to escape. Turning from the state of acceptance and then disillusioned compliance, he begins, from this moment, to move actively toward a game worth playing.

Time and Mortality in *A Farewell to Arms*

D. Quentin Miller

> Surrounded by death in World War I, Frederic Henry cannot help but be aware that every moment may be his last. D. Quentin Miller suggests that despite Henry's best efforts to ignore or escape time, the closer he comes to a battle or other conflict, the more aware of time he is. For most of the novel, specific references to the date or the year are absent. Only when a confrontation with one's mortality is imminent does Hemingway interject a specific time reference. D. Quentin Miller has taught at Gustavus Adolphus College in Saint Peter, Minnesota.

One of the most prominent effects of the Great War was to elicit a widespread confrontation with mortality. The awareness of life's ephemeralness logically involves a heightened consciousness of the passage of time. It is therefore curious that the opening sentence of Hemingway's *A Farewell to Arms* contains an unspecific reference to the year in which the novel begins: "In the late summer of that year we lived in a house in a village that looked across the river and the plain to the mountains." The vague description of the landscape is soon qualified by Italian place names, but the year in which the story takes place is not stated explicitly until close to the end of the book. The concept of time is a problem throughout the story; it saturates the narration at some points, and is notably absent at others.

A Seemingly Endless War

The early chapters contain references to events, such as the battle of the Somme, from which the informed reader can deduce the novel's dates. However, these chapters are largely devoid of specific references to time. Things take

From D. Quentin Miller, "'In the Late Summer of That Year': The Problem of Time in *A Farewell to Arms*," *The Hemingway Review*, vol. 10, no. 2 (Spring 1991), 61–64. Copyright 1991, The Ernest Hemingway Foundation. All rights reserved. Reprinted with the permission of the publisher.

place "after a while" or "in the evening." Frederic describes Rinaldi as his own age, but we are not told what that age is. The days are defined and separated only by the rising and setting of the sun, and are measured in terms of passing seasons rather than by the calendar. When Frederic returns from his leave and tells Rinaldi of his trip, Rinaldi tells him that he talks "like a [railway] time-table." All these circumstances reflect the methodical boredom which the war has produced. In its interminable cycle, it is as if time has ceased to matter.

Hope for the end of the war is expressed in reference to the seasons. Frederic says, "I wished to God it was over though. Maybe it would finish this summer. . . . What was the matter with this war?" The hopelessness of the situation intensifies later, and Frederic makes a futile attempt to quantify the possible duration: "Still nobody was whipping any one on the Western Front. Perhaps wars weren't won any more. Maybe they went on forever. Maybe it was another Hundred Years' War." Catherine expresses the same sentiment: "For three years I looked forward very childishly to the war ending at Christmas. But now I look forward till when our son will be a lieutenant commander." Such exasperation with the apparent interminability of the war causes time to become merely a reminder of death, the probable reason that Frederic refuses to think in terms of specific time when talking about this period of his life.

AFRAID OF TIME

Frederic views the time spent at the front as a wasted period of his life, and he copes with this fact by escaping time's mechanical constraints. While at the front, he cannot completely evade time; there are certain reminders which are necessarily a part of army life, such as 48-hour leaves. For the most part, he manages to suppress specific references to time; however, he cannot effectively do so when faced with danger. The earliest mention of a specific hour comes when he finds out that the offensive is only two days away; typically, Frederic would say he returned to the villa in late afternoon, but with the potentially dangerous offensive at hand, he recalls that it was "five o'clock." He wants to know exactly what time the attack will begin. The possibility of dying has made each minute precious and noteworthy.

This situation is still more apparent during a later period of the war—the Caporetto retreat. Frederic is aware of the imminent life-threatening situation, perhaps more acutely because of having already been wounded once, and references to specific time are again present, even pervasive. He recalls that the retreat begins at three in the morning. He is surprised that the soldier who is to wake him up has no watch, and directs him to a clock on the major's wall. He looks at his own watch frequently, whereas before the retreat we are not even aware that he owns a watch. He is now afraid of time; he allows the men to take food supplies from deserted farmhouses, but when one soldier tries to take a clock, he sharply commands him to "put it back." He even acknowledges time as an enemy; he and the other soldiers "[walk] along together all going fast against time." Earlier he had stated that he did not feel endangered by the war; now he is not so sure, and being confronted with his mortality raises his consciousness of time.

The first successful attempt to escape time comes when he is in the hospital. There he is free from the mundane routine of war; time begins to be measured in terms of meals and accumulated brandy bottles. His relationship with Catherine is blissful, and he feels as though the only time that matters is time spent with her; he says, "All I wanted was to see Catherine. The rest of the time I was glad to kill." Despite this sentiment, he realizes that they cannot live that way forever, and he is enraged when one of the first doctors insists that the success of his leg is "a question of time" and will perhaps take six months to heal; he says, "I can't wait six months to be operated on. My God, doctor, did you ever stay in bed six months?" The doctor asks if he is in a hurry to get back to the front, and he replies, "Why not?" It is important to consider this ambiguity when analyzing the relationship between Frederic and Catherine, for if he were so glad to kill the time when they are apart, he would not want to hasten their separation. It can be inferred from his concern with time that the boredom of the situation exceeds the bliss.

But he again encounters difficulty coping with time when he gets his notice to return to the front, and subsequently must confront the fact that he will have to leave the hospital. He mentions a specific date for the first time in the book, and he has trouble placing himself in time: "The convalescent leave started October fourth when my course was finished.

Three weeks was twenty-one days. That made October twenty-fifth." It is obvious that there are twenty-one days in three weeks; the fact that Frederic states this fact explicitly is evidence that he has not been accustomed to thinking in such terms. The prospect of returning to the front has forced him to be aware of time again because he will have to live without Catherine and return to a potentially life-threatening situation.

The anxiety of separation makes the lovers aware that they only have a certain amount of time together. Immediately after receiving his notice, Frederic notices such details as the fact that Catherine comes on duty specifically at 9:00 a.m. rather than simply "in the morning." Also, he quotes [17th-century English poet Andrew] Marvell just before he is to depart: "But at my back I always hear / Time's winged chariot hurrying near." Taken in its context here, it means much more than Catherine's assessment of it as being "about a girl who wouldn't live with a man." It is an affirmation of time's encroachment on happiness as well as a renewed consciousness of mortality.

TRYING TO ESCAPE TIME

Thus when they are reunited at Stresa after the Caporetto retreat, they must try to escape time and the war. We learn that Frederic makes sure that time will not obtrude; when Count Greffi sends for him, he says, "I looked at my watch; I had taken it off and it was under the pillow." He puts his watch under his pillow to escape time just as he refuses to read the papers in an attempt to escape the war. While in Stresa, he also emphasizes his desire to avoid thinking, including thinking about time. But a flurry of specific references to time which occur just before meeting Count Greffi at five o'clock demonstrate that he is still thinking about it and consequently about mortality, which he discusses at length with Count Greffi.

That evening he is again confronted with danger, as he is informed that he is going to be arrested. His initial response is: "I thought a minute. 'What time do they come to arrest me?'" Time is a concern as they cross the lake; while rowing he is afraid of "losing time." They make it safely to Switzerland and attempt there to lead the timeless life they desired at Stresa. They succeed for a while, living again in terms of seasons, where eating is the only activity worth mentioning. But the impending arrival of "young Catherine" makes time an issue again, and it becomes more important as danger increases. From the time they move to Lausanne until the unsuccessful Caesarian delivery, references to time are frequent. Frederic recalls the exact time the labor begins, the amount of time of each contraction, and the specific times at which he leaves the hospital to eat. He even mentions the year for the first time: "It was March, 1918, and the German offensive had started in France." It is no longer "that year"; the war is not over, but Frederic now considers the date important enough to mention explicitly, even though the date can be deduced by this point in the book from the date of the Caporetto retreat and the length of Catherine's pregnancy.

During Book IV, a sense of immediacy pervades Frederic's thought: "We knew the baby was very close now and it gave us both a feeling as though something were hurrying us and we could not lose any time together." Despite all his efforts, he cannot escape time. He says, "You always feel trapped biologically," partially because he senses his biological clock ticking. His attempt to escape time is linked to his attempt to be a non-thinking creature, and he inevitably fails at both. He thinks about time in terms of mortality, which in turn leads him to think about God. What results is an existential vision where death is the only thing that remains: "Now Catherine would die. That was what you did. You died." The time that he alternately escapes from and dwells upon during the novel parallels his fluctuating consciousness of death and attitude towards religion, and he cannot elude his disturbing thoughts on these matters, despite tremendous efforts to do so.

Enduring Values in the Lost Generation

Joseph Warren Beach

The characters of Hemingway's early novels are members of what his friend and mentor Gertrude Stein called "the lost generation." Such characters live a cynical and world-weary existence, often flouting standard moral conventions. Living in a world torn by warfare, it is a wonder, Joseph Warren Beach asserts, that these men and women have any values at all. Yet Frederic Henry and Catherine Barkley uphold the virtues of love and courage that provide happiness, however temporary, in a world that plays "dirty tricks" on the unlucky. Joseph Warren Beach taught at at the University of Minnesota. His books include *The Technique of Thomas Hardy, Obsessive Images: Symbolism in the Poetry of the 1930's and 1940's*, and *American Fiction, 1920–1940*, from which this excerpt is taken.

It is now time to remark that these reckless and profane young men and women [in Hemingway's earlier novel *The Sun Also Rises*] are the product of a special set of conditions. They are the war generation—the "lost generation," as Gertrude Stein called them. They have lived through times of violence and disorder. They have been disillusioned. They have formed habits suitable to war times and been made unfit for the peaceful routines of civil life. They have been shaken loose from their moorings, saddened in their outlook, made restive and skeptical; above all made unwilling to submit themselves to any authority but of their own creation, to grant any assumptions which they haven't personally tested. This is not Hemingway speaking; these points are nowhere explicitly made in the book. But unless these things are said, the earnest "bourgeois" reader will be un-

Excerpted from Joseph Warren Beach, *American Fiction: 1920–1940*. (New York: Macmillan, 1940.) pp. 83–89.

able to do justice to the strain of earnestness shown by these ne'er-do-wells. There is, of course, a measure of mere swagger and braggadocio in the way they go on—there is something of the show-off in Hemingway's rebels against convention. And it is that which has most impressed a large portion of his readers and imitators. But that is not the whole story with them, any more than it is with any generation of the young who take the bit in their mouth. There is something here of serious independence, and something too, under the flippant disguise, of intellectual criticism. These people are determined not to be the dupes of any stuffed shirt or lawn sleeves.

The amazing thing is, with their start from scratch, that these people go so far on the track of morality—that they recover so much of what is traditional in the civilized code. The case is even more striking in *A Farewell to Arms* (1929). For here there is a positive reaction against something conceived as bad (the War) in favor of something conceived as good, the life together of a man and a woman who love each other.

THE HORROR OF WAR

The Italian action in the World War was notoriously calculating and cold-blooded, not motivated by anything more lofty than materialistic patriotism. The Young American may have entered the ambulance service in Italy as the most available means of serving the cause of "democracy"; but he was early impressed with the seamy side of the whole undertaking as seen from the Italian front. The details given, while meager, are all of a nature to emphasize the mean and unheroic aspects of war; and such discussions of the moral implications of the thing as he hears from others all confirm the impression that this war is no exception to the inherent evil of the institution. The ambulance drivers under his command turn out to be socialists, who see no point in fighting the Austrians but consider that the war was provoked by a class in each country that is stupid and does not realize anything, and that, moreover, makes money out of it. The same view is held by the sensitive and high-minded priest: war is made by the unfeeling and unimaginative, and it would be stopped if the people were organized or if their leaders did not sell them out. Even Rinaldi the surgeon is depressed by the war, though he has been having a fine time in the clinic it provides for him, every day learning to do things smoother and better. Frederick Henry never did feel that it was his war. And when, during the retreat of the army, he is roughly handled by a committee of patriots and has to save his life by swimming down a river, he considers that his obligation ceases. He has done his best to deliver his drivers and his cars to the proper base; and now that they are all lost, he has no further responsibility in this war.

RINALDI VS. THE PRIEST

In one minor but significant way, the badness of war is symbolized by the kind of love that flourishes under these conditions. There are houses for officers and men provided with young girls for the comfort of the warriors. And this is the chief form of relaxation and entertainment available. Any more humane sort of love is precluded by the conditions of the case. This situation is more distressing to the American than to his Italian chum, Rinaldi, the army surgeon; and the latter gets a lot of fun out of the fine good Anglo-Saxon boy "trying to brush away the Villa Rossa from his teeth in the morning, swearing and eating aspirin and cursing harlots."

Frederick is fond of Rinaldi; but in a way he is even more attached to the priest. He stands between the two; he does not share the priest's chastity nor his devotion to God, but he has no inclination to make fun of these, and he feels that the priest "had always known what I did not know and what, when I learned it, I was always able to forget." This is not precisely his chastity or his love of God. But it is, it would appear, his understanding of the essence of love in general. He does not consider that the experiences with women of which Frederick tells him are love. That is only passion and lust. "When you love you wish to do things for. You wish to sacrifice for. You wish to serve." Such a love he will some day find and he will be happy. When Frederick protests that he has always been happy, the priest says, "It is another thing. You cannot know about it unless you have it."

And the priest, as it turns out, is right. When, in his convalescence in the Milan hospital, Frederick finds himself engaged in an affair with his English nurse, this is not a repetition of earlier casual episodes; he is too much concerned with the object of his affection. The carnal element is no less present; but there is added the circumstance that he is devoted to the woman, wishing to do things for her, seeking her well-being. In the hotel at Stresa he has some talk with the aged and wise Count Greffi; and they come, by way of religion, to the subject of values. "What do you value most?" asks the old man. "Someone I love," is the young man's answer. "With me it is the same," says the Count. And while neither of them acknowledges the hold of supernatural faith, the Count insists that love itself is a religious feeling.

Frederick and Catherine are not married. Frederick would like them to be married for her protection. In Italy in time of war there are too many difficulties. Besides, Catherine has no religious faith and regards the matter as indifferent. She protests that she is an honest woman, and that "You can't be ashamed of something if you're only happy and proud of it." The sanctity of marriage—they seem to feel—is not in the religious or legal ceremony but in the essential nature of the relationship.

It may be worth while once again to remind ourselves of the special conditions under which this relationship was formed. I mean the state of things resulting from the War and the presence of these characters in Europe at a great distance from home. They are singularly detached from all that makes for fixity in the social order. The state of war is an abnormal social state. The point is made that both of these persons have cut the ties of family. These people are not of the lost generation in the sense that they have been damaged by the War and rendered unfit for civil life. But they are living in a social no-man's land, where no one is concerned in what they do but themselves.

I have no doubt that many emancipated readers have taken pleasure in the thought of this love affair on the general principle that it is more fun to "live in sin" than to submit to convention. Somewhere Frederick acknowledges to himself that he has the usual masculine reluctance to submit to the yoke. And sentiments like these are natural enough, though they may be shared by shallow people and expressed in cheap and showy ways. There are enough humiliations and hypocrisies and sentimentalisms associated with the state of matrimony fully to justify the pleasure we take in the thought of a moral holiday, not to speak of our quite natural preference for a free and easy life. And the situation presented by Hemingway is plausible enough and significant enough to absolve him from the imputation of any mere desire to exploit the theme of irresponsible love.

A Marriage Sealed in Death

In Switzerland, as the time for Catherine's delivery draws near, it is quite agreed that they will be married after the child is born. For with persons fully persuaded that their attachment is for good and all there would be no point in wishing it otherwise. But this love was destined to be sealed with something more grave even than legal marriage—it was to be sealed with the seal of suffering and death. I used to think that this final episode was artificially attached to the story by Hemingway in order to give it an emotional weight which it did not naturally carry—that it had, in short, a strain of the sentimental or the melodramatic. Later reading has convinced me that the story, from the beginning, is more serious than might be inferred from the tone of irony and understatement that colors the narrative and from the tone of flippancy and emotional reserve that prevails in the dialogue. Once you get the notion that everything has more than its face value, that this is a "religious" passion with which we are concerned, as these things are conceived by the priest and Count Greffi; once you get the notion that Hemingway's generation take some things just as hard as writers with a more eloquent rhetoric, the tragedy of the final chapters follows on with perfect rightness. It may not be necessary to the logic of the story that Catherine should die in childbirth. But is the most effective means that could be devised for demonstrating the seriousness of her lover's feeling. On present reading I find no sentimentalism in the conclusion that is not present in the whole. I am not much inclined to call it sentimental. Let us say rather that Hemingway, in his severely "modern" and unromantic idiom, has given us a view of love as essentially romantic as any of his predecessors in the long line of English novelists.

The tragedy remains, and a certain saturnine attitude toward the whole show. One thing the author lays himself out to exhibit is the pluck of the heroine—the pluck of a healthy organism not intimidated by the complexities and menaces of life. She realizes, however, that life is a battle, that the hostile powers are many, and that it is accordingly important for her and her man not to be divided in their forces. "Because there's only us two and in the world there's all the rest of them. If anything comes between us we're gone and then they have us." "They won't get us," Frederick assures her.

"Because you're too brave. Nothing ever happens to the brave."

LOVE AND COURAGE AS ENDURING VALUES

In one sense this remains true; for so long as they have the strength of their courage and their love, there can be no complete loss, whatever happens. But with the death of Catherine he had not reckoned. Jake in the earlier story [*The Sun Also Rises*] was trying to learn how to live in life. "Maybe if you found out how to live in it you learned what it was all about." But now Frederick realizes that one can never learn how to live in it. The rules are too difficult to learn and the masters of the game too ruthless in their application of the rules. Catherine has been trapped by a biological force. She is going to die as a result of her love. "You died," he says to her in thought. "You did not know what it was all about. You never had time to learn. They threw you in and told you the rules and the first time they caught you off base they killed you." That is his judgment in the face of her imminent death. And hers is "It's just a dirty trick."

It would not be a "modern" novel if this protest were not uttered against the rules of the game. But even so, the reader can hardly feel that he is left with nothing more constructive than the notion of an order given to playing dirty tricks on mortals. Along with that, he is left with certain "values" of which the whole story is a dramatic embodiment—the transcendental values of courage and "love." And these are something, according to this author's formula, to "make you feel good after."

The General Versus the Specific in *A Farewell to Arms*

Floyd C. Watkins

According to Floyd C. Watkins, in *A Farewell to Arms* Hemingway portrays the conflict between an individual's instinctual needs and the generalized patriotism and group mentality that propel men into combat. Watkins analyzes the concluding sections of the novel, including the famous and highly regarded scene describing the retreat from Caporetto. He shows how group responsibilities fade for Frederic and his fellow soldiers, to be replaced by a visceral need to survive and to love. Floyd C. Watkins has taught at Emery University in Georgia. His books include *Talking with Robert Penn Warren, Practical English Handbook,* and *The Flesh and the Word: Eliot, Hemingway, Faulkner.*

Every aspect of the art and the meaning of *A Farewell to Arms* establishes a conflict between the concrete, the particular, the individual on the one hand and the abstract, the general, and the mass on the other. The larger theme is figured in several ways: the individual caught in the toils of the war; lovers trapped by their own bodies or by the mortal world in which they love; the individual's solipsism, and terrible need for religion in a world without belief and without an order or a pattern which might provide evidence of something in which to believe. Plot, image, character, event—the minute details of the novel reflect the whole.

Naïve Patriotism

The themes of love, war, and religion dominate the patterns of meaning in *A Farewell to Arms.* Only one of these is perfectly comprehensible and without mystery—war. Love and religion remain complex, mysterious, inexplicable. An army and battle police can more definitely represent a society than love and a priest can represent the divine and the mystical. One may desert the army and make his separate peace, but he cannot withdraw from his own body without death; nor can he simply by proclamation separate himself from chaos or rule himself outside the theological order. The theme of war in *A Farewell to Arms*, therefore, because of the very nature of the problems involved, most clearly reveals the over-all design of the novel.

Only the naïve patriot in the novel may believe wholeheartedly in the cause of his country. Such a man is Gino, who provokes Frederic to think of his embarrassment at words: "Gino was a patriot, so he said things that separated us sometimes, but he was also a fine boy and I understood his being a patriot." Ettore was worse—"a legitimate hero who bored everyone he met." Gino provides an opportunity for Frederic to examine himself. Until the retreat from Caporetto he is more disturbed by the words than he is by the patriotism which they represent. That he himself was something of an idealist is indicated by his talk with disgruntled soldiers. As concretely as he can, he tells them that "defeat is worse" than war, and again he says, "I believe we should get the war over." But the restraint of these abstractions indicates only the vaguest kind of patriotism. Even these minor symptoms of belief disappear after his desertion, and always they are made to seem insignificant in comparison with the other soldiers' hatred of the war. The triviality of Frederic's little patriotic displays is also made apparent by the contrast with his ardent feelings about his men. Personal relationships are comparable to facts, the words of the senses, the names of places. Under artillery fire, Frederic takes food to his men. Told to wait, he says, "They want to eat." Here are sacrifice, honor, courage; but even to name the virtues is to diminish the force of the deed. If a character used the words, he would be a bore like Gino. A shell hits the group; and Manera, one of the most disgruntled and mutinous of the men, tenderly leads in the rescue of Frederic after he is wounded. One could say of him ... that there is a great difference between his "world pessimism" and his personal loyalty.

THE RETREAT FROM CAPORETTO

The retreat from Caporetto reveals best the difference between the world and the individual. Different episodes in the retreat indicate a change in Frederic's view of the self, the war, and the world. The first of these, the shooting of the sergeant, is the most complex moral situation in the novel; and though it is a key to meaning in *A Farewell to Arms*, it has been ignored in almost all interpretations of the book. Henry's men invite two sergeants to ride in their ambulances during the retreat. From the moment when the two join the ambulance drivers, Hemingway begins preparing for the climactic desertion of the army by Frederic, and he juxtaposes several moral systems: the responsibilities of the individual to himself, to his group of friends, and to his general military or patriotic cause. The whole situation has been interpreted as mere selfish inconsistency on the part of Frederic: "Though he does not hesitate to kill a deserter," writes [critic] Francis Hackett, "he himself deserts when offered the same dose of medicine. . . ." The medicine is the same, but the disease is not. First of all, the sergeants violate the code of a group by eating first without sharing. (Contrast Frederic's carrying food to his men during bombardment.) The sergeants enjoy the ride for a long time, but they are unwilling to share the ill fortunes of the group. When the ambulances are stuck in the mud, the sergeants refuse to push or to cut brush to put under the wheels. Thus they betray those who have helped them and disobey the orders of a superior officer. At a moment of desperate crisis they violate military law as well as the laws of common human decency. Frederic shoots at both as they flee and hits one. At this moment he has two different kinds of justification, but obviously he does not debate his reasons and offer explanations. Later, after his own desertion, he might. Bonello, the most brazen, cocksure, and unpatriotic of Frederic's men, administers a coup de grâce mostly for the pleasure of killing. "'The son of a bitch,' he said. He looked toward the sergeant. 'You see me shoot him, Tenente?'" Bonello and Frederic act with all "the beautiful detachment and devotion to stern justice" of the carabinieri who try to execute Henry later. But they also have a personal and particular justification. What Frederic should have done, indeed, what he would have done, about the sergeants after his own desertion, remains a point more for contemplation than solution.

After the killing of the sergeant all obligations and responsibilities to group and to military cause begin to disappear. Events make personal loyalty seem less meaningful.

Before crossing a bridge, Bonello cares more for his own safety than that of the group: "'It's probably mined,' he says. 'You cross first, Tenente.'" Faith in the general world becomes as meaningless as the words which might describe it. The loyal Aymo is shot by his own countrymen. Words and the world have failed Frederic, and about the death of Aymo he can only say, "He looked very dead. It was raining. I had liked him as well as any one I ever knew. I had his papers in my pocket and would write to his family."

Bonello leaves the group because he wishes to be a prisoner. Piani stays even though he does not believe in the war. He does not wish to leave Frederic. Even before Frederic is finally convinced by the carabinieri that he should make a separate peace, the loyalty of Piani is all that is left to cling to. Personally devoted to Frederic, Piani respectfully calls him "Tenente," but the retreating troops have their own "beautiful detachment and devotion to stern justice." Piani therefore calls his lieutenant by his first name because the men may shoot officers. At this point Frederic still feels enough loyalty to the general situation to voice to Piani his objection to the troops' throwing away their rifles.

At the end of the retreat with the army Frederic encounters the battle police. They have "all the efficiency, coldness, and command of themselves of Italians who are firing and not being fired on." "That beautiful detachment and devotion to stern justice of men dealing in death without being in any danger of it." They still can mouth the abstractions like *in vain*, *glory*, *courage*, and *honor*. One of them refers to "the sacred soil of the fatherland." But these men know nothing about the facts, the concrete actions which the words are supposed to describe. Of all the characters in the novel, they are the best representatives of abstraction and generality.

A STRANGE BAPTISM

To escape execution by the battle police, Frederic jumps into a river and swims to safety. In words that suggest baptism Henry later reflects on his escape: "Anger was washed away in the river along with any obligation." This sentence has been the delight of many critics. First was Malcolm Cowley: "When Frederick [sic] Henry dives into the flooded Tagliamento . . . , he is performing a rite of baptism that prepares us for the new life he is about to lead as a deserter from the Italian army; his act is emotionally significant, but it is a little unconvincing on the plane of action." Acknowledging his indebtedness to Cowley, John W. Aldridge calls the escape in the river "an act of purgation symbolizing the death of the war and the beginning of a new life of love." And Robert Penn Warren refers to "baptism" and "the significance of a rite."

This is, however, a strange kind of baptism. Frederic's mental state does not resemble that which should accompany the Christian sacrament. In the river during his escape he thinks almost as a hunted animal. Even after he has found a hiding place in a railroad car under a canvas with guns, he does not reflect on the battle police, his desertion, his perilous situation, his justification. Before thinking about the general world, he ponders over the performance of his stiff knee. "The head was mine, but not to use, not to think with; only to remember and not too much remember." The ceremony is an ironic parody of baptism, a travesty of the ceremony. The change and dedication that should precede baptism is a change in the appearance of the world, not in Frederic. Saint Paul's blinding light here is the threat of unjust execution. The newly baptized Christian assumes obligations; Frederic now can deny them. It is more initiation than baptism. Instead of subscribing to a new belief in the transcendent life of the spirit, Frederic uses his own personal principles to act in a new way because he has learned new things about the disorder of the world. Not only is he embarrassed at the words *sacred, sacrifice,* and *in vain,* but now he also doubts the existence of the facts that the words might describe. He had seen the sacred implicit in the names of places; but Caporetto can suggest only the profane. Whatever verities there may be exist only in the personal, in the relationship of love, in himself and Catherine.

The escape in the river does almost complete Frederic's knowledge about the war and the great world. "My life used to be full of everything," he tells Catherine. "Now if you aren't with me I haven't a thing in the world." When a friendly bartender asks him why men go to war, Frederic for the first time can reply factually, although he will answer the question only for himself: "I don't know. I was a fool."

THE LOVE THEME

The climactic escape and desertion marks a sharp change in the structure of *A Farewell to Arms.* The style and the general theme are the same but the love of Catherine and Frederic replaces the war as the vehicle of narration and meaning. Before, Frederic had to define the place of the individual in society and the world; the moment of definition came with desertion; now, he and Catherine must define the place of lovers in creation. If the individual can only try and fail to make a separate peace in a world, lovers ultimately can attain only separation and death. Disaster comes early for Catherine and Frederic, but sooner or later, they learn, it comes to all.

But before the death of Catherine and Frederic's realization of the place of love in the world, the two are almost as alone in the mountains of Switzerland as Eve and Adam were in the Garden. And as innocent. Frederic's desertion was but an early bloom on the tree of knowledge. Although *innocence* is an odd word to use in describing Catherine and Frederic, their love in a sense exists apart from the world. "'I wish we could do something really sinful,' Catherine said. 'Everything we do seems so innocent and simple. I can't believe we do anything wrong.'"

The priest describes such a love as that of Catherine and Frederic in terms that are idealistic but not sexual: "When you love you wish to do things for." But this sentence, concrete as it is, borders on abstraction, and the two lovers avoid such statements of what they feel. When Frederic realizes that he loves Catherine, he lets all the meanings remain in physical terms: "Everything turned over inside of me." The lovers' refusal, indeed, inability, to talk about love in terms of the embarrassing words leaves much unsaid, and here may be a reason for what many regard as Hemingway's failure to characterize Catherine. John W. Aldridge, for example, regards the love affair as "strangely inadequate." "Instead of emerging as a human personality," Catherine he believes, "became merely an abstraction. . . ." Hemingway had set himself a difficult task in trying to portray an individual woman who rejects all the words that the women of the world use to describe the *raison d'être* [reason for being] of marriage and womanhood.

After the reality of their love has been expressed by the flesh, marriage becomes a convention, a religious or civil institution, a generalization. Catherine's friend Ferguson accuses Catherine of having no honor, but Ferguson thinks with the immoral world's embarrassing words. Frederic wishes marriage more than Catherine because in the priest's terms he might be doing a thing for the one he loves. In keeping with his rejection of the world, he wishes to be "married privately some way," but Catherine reminds him of the meaninglessness of marriage in the moral terms of the book when she tells him that "There's no way to be married except by church or state." And in a happy moment the concrete good feelings of love are so predominant that Catherine says they are already married—and given a chaotic world like that in this novel, any ceremony would be love's sacrilege.

Love therefore is a refuge from the failure of all generalities. And the world vanishes during the Edenic life in Switzerland. After Catherine and Frederic leave Italy in a small boat on a lake, the two think only of the concrete things of the sensations which they endure and enjoy. There are no thoughts of a separate peace, not even talk about the war. Switzerland is "a grand country," "a splendid country," where "The war seemed as far away as the football games of some one else's college." In Switzerland they eat pretzels, drink beer, enjoy the weather, and read "about disaster." The idyll which Hemingway has written about the days of Catherine and Frederic in the mountains is one of the simplest and most beautiful passages in his works.

But the world cannot be denied. In *A Farewell to Arms* it works out destinies with little or no regard for the meanings of the embarrassing words it uses. The individual is not freely given that prerogative of decision. The hard paradox is that Frederic on the one hand has every right to say farewell to arms; but the world will not let him exercise the right with impunity. Though there be chaos and evil, the individual must act in the terms of duty and honor. Already years before *For Whom the Bell Tolls* Hemingway is aware that no man can be an island. But a chaotic world still forces a man to try to be an island, and paradoxically even as he flees from evil he is wrong in his flight. Trapped in a mortal world, faced with social obligations, man must accept. There is no way to sign a separate peace with all creation and life itself. Robert Penn Warren describes well the doom of the lovers: "the attempt to find a substitute for universal meaning in the limited meaning of the personal relationship is doomed to failure." Love, which helped to carry them out of the world, makes them return when Catherine goes to the hospital in Lausanne to bear her child. Always the baby reminds them that they cannot deny the press of the world. When the time of birth is near, Catherine and Frederic share a "feeling as though something were hurrying us and we could not lose any time together." Whether Hemingway or Henry regards the baby as the agent of the world or whether Henry's attitude is merely that of a father-to-be who does not yet know and love his child is never clear. In a sense Frederic and Catherine have even been isolated from their own unborn child. And he is so much worried about her that he has no time for concern about the baby. After Catherine and the baby die, Frederic still cannot define his role in creation. He knows that in a sense the baby also has been "biologically trapped." If he thought in Christian terms he would recognize the biological trap as mortality, the fall of man. And the trap indicates that Nature—or God if there is One—rather than man brought death into the world and all our woe. "Poor little kid. I wished the hell I had been choked like that." Though he has no religion, he prays for Catherine and recognizes that the baby should be baptized.

By this time the words *glorious* and *sacred* are meaningless as well as embarrassing. The particular facts to which one may cling are that the words mean little and sometimes nothing in the world, that the individual cannot speak the words, but that he must act with sacrifice and courage and pity and pride. He must endure in a world without explanations.

In the war Frederic learns that the individual is trapped in a society that mouths words without knowing the meanings. Only the relationships between individuals in small groups can be true. In his love affair Frederic learns that he is mortal, that he is "biologically trapped." In religion he never learns anything. From the beginning to the end of the novel he yearns for a faith like that of the priest. Like the words, religion remains vague and abstract. The ultimate in Frederic's knowledge of religious things is expressed by Count Greffi, who tells him that love is a "religious feeling." But religion is too vague for Catherine who tells Frederic that he is her religion. Hemingway's doomed lovers never know whether love is a substitute for religion because there is no God or whether it is a concrete and ideal experience which may enable them to become very devout when they are old. Even in religion they maintain a world skepticism and a personal cheeriness. Frederic's lack of faith allows him to blaspheme although he prays in moments of fear and he cannot put away religious things.

In *A Farewell to Arms,* style and the major subjects of the novel (war, love, religion) form an almost perfect harmony in the rejection of the general and vague and the acceptance only of the particular, the things of the senses, the knowable. Both style and theme reject the words which do not refer to a material thing. In historical terms *A Farewell to Arms* is very much a book of its time. The two lovers desire what [British mathematician, logician, and philosopher] Alfred North Whitehead has described as an *"Order of Nature...."* "It does not matter what men say in words," Whitehead wrote in 1925, "so long as their activities are controlled by settled instincts. The words may ultimately destroy the instincts." He might have been writing of Catherine and Frederic when he wrote that the "new tinge to modern minds is a vehement and passionate interest in the relation of general principles to irreducible and stubborn facts." Hemingway and Frederic and Catherine admitted the possibility of the existence of principles and mind and spirit, even with capital letters, but for author and characters the instincts could not be expressed in the embarrassing words which have been destroyed. Words change in every age; but in Hemingway's early career, he said, "words we knew were barred to us, and we had to fight for a single word...." In these respects *A Farewell to Arms* is one of the best manifestations of an attitude in an age, but, more significantly, Hemingway has created a novel that will be a lasting work of art. Most of Catherine's and Frederic's soul-searchings resemble those of any thinking individual in any period, and they are embodied in a vehicle so appropriate to the theme that style and subject become indistinguishable and inseparable.

CHAPTER 4
The Novelist's Technique

The Original Opening of *A Farewell to Arms*

Bernard Oldsey

Hemingway was known for heavily revising his work. In the following article, Bernard Oldsey cites a manuscript that he claims represents the earliest known beginning of A Farewell to Arms. *This opening corresponds to what is now chapters 13 and 14 of the novel, when the wounded protagonist arrives at the hospital in Milan. Although starting in the middle of the story was typical of Hemingway's technique, doing so would have required extensive use of flashback. So Hemingway apparently made the decision to begin his story at a much earlier point in time, and this decision paved the way for the masterful and poetic prose with which the novel begins. Bernard Oldsey has taught at West Chester State College in Pennsylvania. His books include* The Art of William Golding *and* Hemingway's Hidden Craft: The Writing of *A Farewell to Arms.*

One of the reasons *A Farewell to Arms* is critically esteemed is that it is a well-structured novel possessed of a poetically evocative opening and a dramatically understated conclusion. But before Ernest Hemingway reached the beginning and ending of the novel as eventually published, he was beset by considerable difficulties. These were not new with him: as [English novelist] George Eliot once confided in correspondence, "beginnings are always troublesome" and "conclusions are the weak point of most authors." Nor was he lacking in experience in dealing with a troublesome beginning. The story of how [American novelist; Hemingway's friend] F. Scott Fitzgerald helped him through the initial difficulties of *The Sun Also Rises* is now well known. . . . The story of how Hemingway wrote and rewrote the troublesome conclusion of *A*

Excerpted from Bernard Oldsey, "The Genesis of *A Farewell to Arms*," *Studies in American Fiction*, vol. 5, no. 2 (Autumn 1977), pp. 175–83. Reprinted with the permission of the publisher. (Footnotes in the original have been omitted in this reprint.)

Farewell to Arms is also widely but less accurately known in respect to the manuscript facts (although estimates have varied widely, there are over forty extant forms of that conclusion in the Hemingway Collection). What is not known is that Hemingway made an even more drastic adjustment in the opening of *A Farewell to Arms* than he did in *The Sun Also Rises* and with even more radical results.

An Earlier Version of the Novel's Beginning

No one has mentioned this radical change before because evidence of it was not known to exist. However, the Hemingway Collection, housed in the John F. Kennedy Library, now includes certain items not listed in Young and Mann's pioneer inventory, *The Hemingway Manuscripts*. . . . Among these is a two-chapter fragment which is vital to any discussion of the means by which *A Farewell to Arms* was composed and constructed. This remarkable Item-240 [the library's catalogue number for the manuscript] is an early (perhaps the original) opening of the novel, and it corresponds with a section some eighty pages within the novel as published, corresponding with chapters XIII and XIV. What this indicates is that Hemingway composed the opening and the eleven other essential chapters that constitute Book One of the novel as an afterthought, an artistically excellent and serendipitous [arrived at by chance] afterthought.

Item-240, unfortunately undated, consists of two chapters done in the author's hand. The first chapter of eight pages describes the arrival of the wounded protagonist in Milan, where there is much difficulty in getting him to an upper floor in an elevator, and where a flustered nurse is unprepared for this first, unexpected, American casualty. In substance this manuscript chapter corresponds with Chapter XIII of the published novel, although varying in some detail. The second manuscript chapter of six pages describes the protagonist awakening the next morning in the hospital and being attended to by nurses. In substance it corresponds with Chapter XIV of the novel, although varying remarkably in detail of primary importance to the eventual plot.

It might be best to summarize and then to explain the facts that indicate Item-240 is either the original or at least a very early version of the beginning of *A Farewell to Arms*: (1) although the first manuscript chapter is unnumbered, the other is designated "Chapter 2" in the author's hand; (2) at this stage of development the protagonist is named not Frederic Henry but *E*mmett *H*ancock (noteworthy when compared with *E*rnest *H*emingway); (3) although "Chapter 2" contains attending nurses, it does not contain anyone resembling Catherine Barkley, or even the name; it has no reunion scene between the wounded protagonist and his inamorata (as of course Chapter XIV of the novel does); and (4) Item-240 is rougher in prose style and sketchier in detail than Chapters XIII and XIV. Separately each of these facts is indicative; together they represent good evidence that Item-240 is an "ur-opening" [earliest opening] of the novel. . . .

Chapter XIV of *A Farewell to Arms* dramatizes the reunion of Frederic and Catherine Barkley whose affair, as Rinaldi might put it, "has made progress." Item-240, as previously stated, simply has no Catherine and no reunion of wounded soldier and his girl. The pertinent "Chapter 2" does mention an older, incapable nurse by the name of Miss Walker, who survives in the novel. And it contains an American girl—the first American that Emmett Hancock "had seen for a year"—but she is, alas, doomed to compositional limbo. Described as short, dressed in white, possessed of "dark hair" and "red lips," this countrywoman of Hancock's is an impossible imaginative stretch away from the Scottish Catherine Barkley, who, when she finally is born into the world of books, is "blonde," "quite tall," with "tawny skin and gray eyes."

Item-240 reflects much the same sketchiness and indecision in respect to prose quality and narrative detail as it does in respect to characterization. And although this early beginning of the novel cannot be reproduced here, any but the most superficial examination of this portion of the manuscripts would substantiate the report made here. No reader of Hemingway would describe Item-240 as a polished piece of the author's prose nor, at the same time, doubt that it stands as the early basis of a somewhat reworked Chapter XIII and a drastically reworked Chapter XIV.

PROBLEMS WITH THE ORIGINAL BEGINNING

If the author had chosen to continue with the material of Item-240 as the beginning of this novel, *A Farewell to Arms* would obviously have turned into a considerably different work. But it would have been in keeping with a number of his narratives which begin *in medias res* [in the middle of things] with the protagonist already wounded, suffering, incapacitated, or recuperating (including "In Another Country," "The Gambler, The Nun and The Radio," "The Snows of Kilimanjaro," and, in a somewhat different vein, "A Way You'll Never Be," "Big Two-Hearted River," and *The Sun Also Rises*). In this instance, however, Hemingway would have encountered a problem in narrative strategy much akin to that which confronted Fitzgerald some years later in trying to decide whether to begin *Tender is the Night* with Rosemary Hoyt's story or the Divers' (two versions of the novel exist and help prove the difficulty of such opening problems). Hemingway would have had to devise a method to filter in the exposition and introductory narrative material—of prime importance to theme, mode, and character development—which are now contained in the first twelve chapters of *A Farewell to Arms*. In other words, he would have had to eliminate completely, or treat through flashback, the actual wounding of the protagonist; and he would have had to introduce the priest, Rinaldi, and Catherine (or again try cumbersome flashbacks) in Milan during the period of hospitalization and recuperation.

It is almost impossible to say how and when Hemingway reached his final decision on structuring the novel: to begin at the Isonzo Front rather than in Milan. Neither biographical data nor manuscript materials provide the answer. The same Fitzgerald who made brilliant editorial recommendations on the opening of *The Sun Also Rises* also made excellent recommendations on this new novel; yet the extant manuscript of his nine pages of notes to Hemingway on *A Farewell to Arms* contains nothing about the opening of the novel—nothing, strangely enough, about anything in the first twelve chapters. And the same Maxwell Perkins who was Hemingway's editor at Scribner's, and did so much to help shape [American novelist] Thomas Wolfe's voluminous outpourings into something resembling novels, was of no discernible help in this instance. In fact, his letters show a wondrous lack of knowledge about what Hemingway was up to during the 1928 compositional period. As late as April 19, 1928, Perkins was still wondering whether Hemingway might have some kind of manuscript "for the fall," and then seems surprisedly overwhelmed by his first and second readings of the novel in typescript on his visit to the author in Key West in 1929. The important thing is that Hemingway, even before reaching what was for him often the second stage of composition (typescript), had done a manuscript version of the opening much as it is now, beginning with the familiar sentence "In the late summer of that year we lived in a house in a village that looked across the river and the plain to the mountains." At this stage of the composition there are the marks of numerous deletions and insertions and the materials of Chapter I have not as yet been rounded into completion nor have they been separated from the materials of Chapter II and made into a discrete unit. Nonetheless, Hemingway had by this time made an immense advance in starting and structuring his novel.

A Memorable and Poetic Opening

The first sentence of *A Farewell to Arms* may not be as memorable as [*Moby Dick*'s] "Call me Ishmael" or [*A Tale of Two*

The Famous First Paragraph of *A Farewell to Arms*

Noted novelist and essayist Joan Didion details the deceptive simplicity of the beginning of A Farewell to Arms.

In the late summer of that year we lived in a house in a village that looked across the river and the plain to the mountains. In the bed of the river there were pebbles and boulders, dry and white in the sun, and the water was clear and swiftly moving and blue in the channels. Troops went by the house and down the road and the dust they raised powdered the leaves of the trees. The trunks of the trees too were dusty and the leaves fell early that year and we saw the troops marching along the road and the dust rising and leaves, stirred by the breeze, falling and the soldiers marching and afterward the road bare and white except for the leaves.

A Mysterious Simplicity

So goes the famous first paragraph of Ernest Hemingway's "A Farewell to Arms,". . . That paragraph, which was published in 1929, bears examination: four deceptively simple sentences, one hundred and twenty-six words, the arrangement of which remains as mysterious and thrilling to me now as it did when I first read them, at twelve or thirteen, and imagined that if I studied them closely enough and practiced hard enough I might one day arrange one hundred and twenty-six words myself. Only one of the words has three syllables. Twenty-two have two. The other hundred and three have one. Twenty-four of the words are "the," fifteen are "and." There are four commas. The liturgical cadence of the paragraph derives in part from the placement of the commas (their presence in the second and fourth sentences, their absence in the

Cities'] "It was the best of times, it was the worst of times" or [*Anna Karenina*'s] "Happy families are all alike. . . ." The first chapter, however, is one of the most celebrated opening chapters in American fiction, with much of the commentary on it, like that of [literary critics] Edmund Wilson and Ford Madox Ford, concentrating on the pureness of its English prose, the tessellated words standing out as clearly as white stones in a stream. No one seems to have noticed that this two-page chapter of highly cadenced prose has more in common with French literary methods than it does with any other introductory methods in the English or American novel. To find anything like it in intent we must go to [French novelist] Marcel Proust's multi-volumed *À la recher-*

first and third), but also from that repetition of "the" and of "and," creating a rhythm so pronounced that the omission of "the" before the word "leaves" in the fourth sentence ("and we saw the troops marching along the road and the dust rising and leaves, stirred by the breeze, falling") casts exactly what it was meant to cast, a chill, a premonition, a foreshadowing of the story to come, the awareness that the author has already shifted his attention from late summer to a darker season. The power of the paragraph, offering as it does the illusion but not the fact of specificity, derives precisely from this kind of deliberate omission, from the tension of withheld information. In the late summer of *what* year? *What* river, *what* mountains, *what* troops?

A Detached Point of View

This was a writer who had in his time made the English language new, changed the rhythms of the way both his own and the next few generations would speak and write and think. The very grammar of a Hemingway sentence dictated, or was dictated by, a certain way of looking at the world, a way of looking but not joining, a way of moving through but not attaching, a kind of romantic individualism distinctly adapted to its time and source. If we bought into those sentences, we would see the troops marching along the road, but we would not necessarily march with them. We would report, but not join. We would make, as Nick Adams made in the Nick Adams stories and as Frederic Henry made in "A Farewell to Arms," a separate peace: "In the fall the war was always there, but we did not go to it any more."

Joan Didion, "Last Words," *New Yorker*, November 9, 1998, pp 74-75.

ché du temps perdu, which begins with a poetic prelude meant to establish the ambience and the imagistic and structural pattern for that entire work. "L'ouverture," as the introduction is called, is an extended incantation that summons up the past—of flowers, paths, place names, music, people, of madeleine and tea—which unfolds into the fullness of seven volumes.

While this overture of Proust's is sixty pages long, Hemingway's in *A Farewell to Arms* is typical of him in that it is compressed into a mere two pages; but both writers, in proportion to their respective works, were using similar orchestration and both were relying on a method of composition that had been well known in France from the middle of the nineteenth century on—the *poème en prose* [prose-poem].

Whether Hemingway deliberately, consciously used the prose-poem method in composing Chapter I of *A Farewell to Arms* is impossible to say. We might remember, though, that this was the Hemingway who served much of his literary apprenticeship in Paris, who utilized Proust and Villon in writing "The Snows of Kilimanjaro," and who considered using a title from [French novelist Gustave] Flaubert, *The Sentimental Education of Frederick Henry*, for *A Farewell to Arms*. This was the same Hemingway who wrote and spoke French and Spanish with considerable fluency, who contributed heavily cadenced lines of verse to American and European journals, and who moreover produced something remarkably like prose poems in those compressed and cadenced paragraphs and sketches that comprise [his earlier work] *in our time*.

It remains for someone to do a thorough study of Hemingway's debt to French literary examples and methods, particularly the *poème en prose* approach. Here the concern is mainly with the manner in which he used such a method to form an introduction. Published two years before *A Farewell to Arms*, "In Another Country" employs this technique so admirably that Fitzgerald judged its opening paragraph one of the finest prose pieces he had ever read. In many respects, that paragraph (which begins "In the fall the war was always there, but we did not go to it any more," and then in a hundred words previews the entire story, imagistically and thermometrically) is the artistic precursor of the opening chapter of *A Farewell to Arms*. Both are English-language approximations of the *poème en prose* method of investing a paragraph, or a series of tightly linked paragraphs, with many of the qualities of modern poetry—such as an insistent cadence, a concatenation of images and potential symbols, and what T.S. Eliot named the objective correlative. These poetic qualities become even more discernible when the opening paragraph is arranged into one of many possible verse presentations:

> In the late summer of that year
> We lived in a house in a village
> That looked across the river and the plain
> To the mountains.
> In the bed of the river there were pebbles
> And boulders, dry and white in the sun,
> And the water was clear and swiftly moving
> And blue in the channels.
> Troops went by the house and down the road
> And the dust they raised
> Powdered the leaves of the trees.
> The trunks of the trees too were dusty
> And the leaves fell early that year
> And we saw the troops marching along the road
> And the dust rising and leaves,
> Stirred by the breeze,
> Falling
> And the soldiers marching
> And afterward the road bare and white
> Except for the leaves.

STRUCTURE OF THE NOVEL

Chapter I of *A Farewell to Arms* consists of five such prose-poem paragraphs arranged in seasonal progression—summer dominating the first two and a half paragraphs, fall the next paragraph and a half, and winter the last paragraph (of two ironically balanced sentences). Its primary images cluster around the weather, the topography, and the historical fact of war. Thus: *sun, dust, leaves* [dropping], *rich crops, green branches* [cut], *rain, mud, permanent rain* and accompanying *cholera; river, plain, mountains, boulders, valley, vineyards; troops, artillery, motor-tractors, ammunition, rifles, cartridges.* It might be said that Hemingway here simply did what scores of WWI novelists did in setting the scene for a war story; but none of the others (not even the poet-novelist Richard Aldington in his powerfully written *Death of a Hero*) approaches Hemingway in the poetic projection of major motifs through an introductory chapter.

From their source here in the opening chapter, these motif-rays shine throughout the novel, providing unity and *claritas* [clarity]. To considerable extent, Carlos Baker has shown how this is so in his study of symbolic motifs, represented by the initially mentioned mountains and plains, in terms of what happens in the highlands and lowlands throughout the novel. But we could also consider how the introductory "river" leads to the many watery scenes within the novel in which the protagonist is wounded, in which he cleanses himself of hatred and escapes from the front, and then (by another body of water, Lago Maggiore) escapes to Switzerland, where he and Catherine live in a house where they look out over Lake Geneva. Or we could consider the motif elements of the weatherscape in this remarkable opening—where the green leaves turn dusty and then fall, where the green branches are cut, where the rain leads to cholera and death. Even Catherine Barkley's deadly pregnancy in the rain is prefigured in Chapter I as the troops, "muddy and wet in their capes," moving toward combat, carry cartridge-boxes which "bulged forward under the capes so that the men, passing on the road, marched as though they were six months gone with child."

Structurally, as well as imagistically, this poetic opening of *A Farewell to Arms* is remarkable in previewing the entire work, particularly in respect to the insistence on temporal and dramatic demarcation. The novel covers approximately two years in the narrative proper and divides its action into five books which closely approximate the acts of classical tragedy. The first chapter, which might be called "The Masque of the Wet Death," covers about a year and is arranged in three "acts" according to the seasons. Act I, Summer, consists mainly of description and exposition with comment on troop movement. It merges with Act II, Fall, when the leaves drop and the trees turn black: now the heavy-laden troops move to the combat zone, and the little King and his generals dash back and forth in small gray motor-cars. Act III, Winter, is a truncated allegoristic conclusion charged with irony as death arrives in unexpected form: "At the start of the winter came the permanent rain and with the rain came the cholera. But it was checked and in the end only seven thousand died of it in the army." The conclusion of the novel partakes of this same ironic entrance of death in nonmilitary form as Catherine dies in that civil bastion of security, Switzerland.

HEMINGWAY'S SENSE OF COMPOSITION

Hemingway showed good compositional sense in cutting the first two pages of the novel away from those which now constitute Chapter II and making them into a separate chapter. Actually, these first two pages might have been designated as "L'ouverture" or "Prelude" or simply "Introduction," because they do form a chapter unlike any other in the entire novel. This is true not only because of its poetic intensity, its thematic implicativeness, its dramatic unity, but also because of its special narrative viewpoint. Although the remainder of the novel is told from Frederic Henry's first-person-singular point of view, Chapter I is narrated from a first-person-plural point of view. This is a special "we" in that it is not all inclusive, or editorial for that matter. It does not signify "we the soldiers" but rather "we the non-combatants, the onlookers not as yet engaged in action," the "we looking across the river and the plain to the mountains," the "we watching troops and King going by," the "we hearing that things are going very badly, and observing what the cholera can accomplish." This same partial "we" reaches over into Chapter II ("we crossed the river in August and lived in a house in Gorizia"), where it modulates to "I" in the first paragraph and finally gives way to Frederic Henry's first-person-singular viewpoint at the beginning of the third paragraph. Here his personal story begins with the scene in which he watches the priest approach in the falling snow.

So the novel begins with a nearly panoramic view which is then changed, in the manner of a camera zooming in for a close-up of Frederic Henry, who then narrates as a singular being. On occasion, however, the novelist-director moves back to that larger view implied by the "we" method of narration. He does this, for example, in the famous speech on patriotic abstractions, where the author shifts from "I" back to "we": "*I* did not say anything. *I* was always embarrassed by the words sacred, glorious, and sacrifice, and the expression in vain. *We* had heard them, sometimes standing in the rain. . . ." But that view is temporary and in the same passage gives way to "you," another large frame of reference, as in "There were many words that *you* could not stand," which in turn brings the view back to *I*, Frederic Henry (p. 191; italics added).

In poetic method, dramatic structure, and narrative

overview, Chapter I stands out as one of the finest pieces of prefatory composition in all fiction. Here Hemingway displays his considerable skill in employing literary reflectors. Somehow he found ways of making titles, epigraphs [quotations at the beginning of literary works], prefaces, interfacing sketches, and envoys [short concluding remarks] (like "L'envoi" at the end of *In Our Time*) reflect powerful lights on the main narrative body....

When Maxwell Perkins wrote Hemingway (Feb. 27, 1929) about the title of *A Farewell to Arms*, he said, "I think it is a very good one indeed, though it is one of those titles that is better after you read the book.... But even at first sight it is a fine title." His words would apply equally well if *Chapter I* were substituted for *title*. This overture of a chapter is good at first sight but it is "even better after you read the book." In fact, it deserves to be read again, and perhaps again, for among other things it illustrates the genesis and unity of the novel, showing how its ending was in its beginning, or "beginnings."

Two Plots in *A Farewell To Arms*

Philip Young

One of Hemingway's premiere critics finds *A Farewell To Arms* to be a combination of two earlier Hemingway plots, the love plot and the war plot, both of which Hemingway earlier addressed in the short story volume, *In Our Time*. These two plots merge to suggest a sense of doom, symbolized throughout by rain, that culminates in the novel's ending. Frederic is trapped either socially (by war) or biologically (by the deaths of his future wife and child). Though the novel has many elements that are more romantic than realistic, it is ultimately the truthfulness of *A Farewell to Arms* that emerges. Philip Young has taught at Penn State University. In addition to several books on Hemingway, he has written *Three Bags Full: Essays in American Fiction* and *The Private Melville*.

A Farewell to Arms (1929), which borrows its title from a poem of that name by George Peele, reverts to the war and supplies background for *The Sun Also Rises*. For the germs of both of its plots, a war plot and a love plot, it reaches back to [Hemingway's book of short stories] *In Our Time*. An outline of the human arms in the novel is to be found among these early stories in a piece called "A Very Short Story." This sketch, less than two pages long, dealt quickly, as the novel does extensively, with the drinking and love-making in an Italian hospital of an American soldier, wounded in the leg, and a nurse, and had told of their love and their wish to get married. But where the book ends powerfully with the death in childbirth of the woman, the story dribbled off in irony. The lovers parted, the soldier leaving for home to get a job so that he could send for his sweetheart. Before long, however, the nurse wrote that she had a new lover who was going to marry her, though he never did; and then, shortly after receiving the letter, the soldier "contracted gonorrhea from a sales girl in a loop department store while riding in a taxicab through Lincoln Park."

THE WAR PLOT

The war plot of *A Farewell to Arms*, on the other hand, is a greatly expanded version of that Chapter VI sketch in which Nick was wounded and made his separate peace—with Rinaldi, who also appears in the longer work. This wound, which got Nick in the spine, and "I" in the knee, and emasculated Jake, has returned to the knee, which is where Hemingway was most badly hit. Then the same story is rehearsed again in lengthened form. Recuperated enough to return to action after another convalescence in Milan, Lt. Frederic Henry becomes bitter about the society responsible for the war and, caught up in the Italian retreat from Caporetto, he breaks utterly with the army in which he is an officer. And this is again the old protagonist [of Hemingway's earlier works], who cannot sleep at night for thinking—who must not use his head to think with, and will absolutely have to stop it. He is also the man who, when he does sleep, has nightmares, and wakes from them in sweat and fright, and goes back to sleep in an effort to stay outside his dreams.

Unlike Jake Barnes [the protagonist of *The Sun Also Rises*], however, Frederic Henry participates fully in the book's action, and as a person is wholly real. But he is also a little more than that, for just as the response of Americans of the period to the aimless and disillusioned hedonism of Jake and his friends indicated that some subtle chord in them had been struck, so something in the evolution of Frederic Henry from complicity in the war to bitterness and escape has made him seem, though always himself, a little larger than that, too. Complicity, bitterness, escape—a whole country could read its experience, Wilson to Harding, in his, and it began to become clear that in Hemingway as elsewhere "hero" meant not simply "protagonist" but a man who stands for many men. Thus it is that when historians of various kinds epitomize the temper of the American Twenties and a reason for it the adventures of that lieutenant come almost invariably to mind. And also, since these things could hardly be said better, his words:

> I was always embarrassed by the words sacred, glorious, and sacrifice and the expression in vain. We had heard them,

sometimes standing in the rain almost out of earshot, so that only the shouted words came through ... now for a long time, and I had seen nothing sacred, and the things that were glorious had no glory and the sacrifices were like the stockyards at Chicago if nothing was done with the meat except to bury it.... Abstract words such as glory, honor, courage, or hallow were obscene....

It is on the implications of these sentiments, and in order to escape a certain death which he has not deserved, that Henry finally acts. He jumps in a river and deserts: the hell with it. It was an unforgettable plunge.

THE FIRST TRUE HEMINGWAY HEROINE

Memorable too, in her devotion and her ordeal—though much less memorable, and much less real—is Henry's English mistress. Idealized past the fondest belief of most people, and even the more realistic wishes of some, compliant, and bearing unmistakable indications of the troubles to come when she will appear as mistress of heroes to come,

THE SOURCE OF HEMINGWAY'S TITLE

Hemingway took the title of his novel from a poem by sixteenth-century poet George Peele.

Farewell to Arms
To Queen Elizabeth

His golden locks time hath to silver turned;
  O time too swift, O swiftness never ceasing!
His youth 'gainst time and age hath ever spurned,
  But spurned in vain; youth waneth by increasing:
Beauty, strength, youth, are flowers but fading seen;
Duty, faith, love, are roots, and ever green.

His helmet now shall make a hive for bees;
  And, lovers' sonnets turned to holy psalms,
A man-at-arms must now serve on his knees,
  And feed on prayers, which are age's alms:
But though from court to cottage he depart,
His saint is sure of his unspotted heart.

And when he saddest sits in homely cell,
  He'll teach his swains this carol for a song:
'Blest be the hearts that wish my sovereign well,
  Curst be the souls that think her any wrong.'
Goddess, allow this aged man his right,
To be your beadsman now, that was your knight.

Helen Gardner, ed., *The New Oxford Book of English Verse, 1250–1950*. New York: Oxford University Press, 1972, p. 97.

Catherine Barkley has at least some character in her own right, and is both the first true "Hemingway heroine," and the most convincing one. Completely real, once again and at once, are the minor characters—especially Rinaldi, the ebullient Italian doctor, and the priest, and Count Greffi, the ancient billiard player, and the enlisted ambulance drivers.

Hemingway's Style

Chiefly, again, it is their speech which brings these people to life and keeps them living. The rest of the book, however, is less conversational in tone than before, and in other ways the writing is changed a little. The sentences are now longer, even lyrical, on occasion, and, once in a while, experimental, as Hemingway, not content to rest in the style that had made him already famous, tries for new effects, and does not always succeed. Taken as a whole, however, his prose has never been finer or more finished than in this novel. Never have those awesome, noncommittal understatements, which say more than could ever be written out, been more impressive. The book has passages which rate with the hardest, cleanest and most moving in contemporary literature.

Rain as a Symbol of Disaster

The novel has one stylistic innovation that is important to it. This is the use of an object, rain, in a way that cannot be called symbolic so much as portentous. Hemingway had used water as a metaphoric purge of past experience before, and so Henry's emergence from the river into a new life, as from a total immersion, was not new. What is new in *A Farewell to Arms* is the consistent use of rain as a signal of disaster. Henry, in his practical realism, professes a disbelief in signs, and tells himself that Catherine's vision of herself dead in the rain is meaningless. But she dies in it and actually, glancing back at the end, one sees that a short, introductory scene at the very start of the book had presented an ominous conjunction of images—rain, pregnancy and death—which set the mood for all that was to follow, prefigured it and bound all the ends of the novel into a perfect and permanent knot.

This is really the old "pathetic fallacy" [giving human traits to inanimate nature] put to new use, and—since there is no need to take it scientifically or philosophically, but simply as a subtle and unobtrusive device for unity—quite an acceptable one, too. Good and bad weather go along with good and bad moods and events. It is not just that, like everyone, the characters respond emotionally to conditions of atmosphere, light and so on, but that there is a correspondence between these things and their fate. They win when it's sunny, and lose in the rain.

Thus, then, the weather, which as both omen and descriptive background (made once again to count for something) is a matter of style, cannot be extricated from the book's plot, or structure. This is of course built on the two themes involved in the ambiguity of "arms," which are developed and intensified together, with alternating emphasis, until at the extremity of one the hero escapes society, and the heroine everything. Despite the frequency with which they appear in the same books, the themes of love and war are really an unlikely pair, if not indeed—to judge from the frequency with which writers fail to wed them—quite incompatible. But in Hemingway's novel their courses run straight and exactly, though subtly, parallel, and he has managed to fuse them. In his affair with the war Henry goes from desultory participation to serious action and a wound, and then through his recuperation in Milan to a retreat which leads to his desertion. His relationship with Catherine Barkley undergoes six precisely corresponding stages—from a trifling sexual affair to actual love and her conception, and then through her confinement in the Alps to a trip to the hospital which leads to her death. By the end of Hemingway's novel, when the last farewell is taken, the two stories are as one, in the point that is made very clear, lest there be any sentimental doubt about it, that life, both social and personal, is a struggle in which the Loser Takes Nothing, either.

This ideology, which is the novel's, has two related aspects which are implicit in the united elements of the plot. In the end, a man is trapped. He is trapped biologically—in this case by the "natural" process that costs him his future wife in the harrowing scenes at the hospital, and is trapped by society—at the end of a retreat, where you take off or get shot. Either way it can only end badly, and there are no other ways. How you will get it, though, depends on the kind of person you are:

> If people bring so much courage to this world the world has to kill them to break them, so of course it kills them. The world breaks everyone and afterward many are strong at the broken places. But those that will not break it kills. It kills the very good and the very gentle and the very brave impartially. If you are none of these you can be sure that it will kill you too but there will be no special hurry.

A Romantic Novel

It does not really matter very much that there is something a little romantic about this passage, perhaps the finest in all of Hemingway, or that the novel is a romantic one as a whole. It must be just about the most romantic piece of realistic fiction, or the most realistic romance, in our literature. Henry's love affair, which blossoms glamorously from the mud of the war, is but the most striking of several factors which go together to make his war a remarkably pleasant one, as wars go, and much more attractive than wars actually are. The lieutenant has a somewhat special time of it, with orderlies and porters and little or no trouble with superiors, and good wine and good food and a lot of free time in which to enjoy them. But it is not important that these aspects of his army experience are highly untypical. Nor does it matter on the other hand that women usually survive childbirth, and many men are discharged from armies in good shape, and then life goes on much as before. What matters instead is that this time Hemingway has made his story, and the attitudes it enacts, persuasive and compelling within the covers of his book. And after we have closed the covers there is no inclination to complain that this was after all, no literal transcription of reality which exaggerated neither the bitter nor the sweet. It was rather an intensification of life. Willingly or not, disbelief is suspended before a vision that overrides objections, withers preconceptions and even memory and imposes itself in their place.

The Truth of the Novel

This novel has the last word, always. Catherine Barkley, as it happened, was very good, very gentle, very brave. Unlike the hero, who broke and survived to become eventually quite strong, she would not break and so she was killed. It was very likely in rebuttal to the people who rejected the pessimism of this denouement that Hemingway pointed out three years later, in *Death in the Afternoon*, that love stories do not end happily in life, either:

> There is no lonelier man in death, except the suicide, than that man who has lived many years with a good wife and then outlived her. If two people love each other there can be no happy end to it....

The Symbolic Structure of *A Farewell To Arms*

Carlos Baker

Arguably Hemingway's foremost literary critic and biographer, Carlos Baker considers the two organizing symbols of the novel, the mountains and the plain. Hemingway juxtaposes these landscapes in the novel's opening and carries the motif through to the book's conclusion. The mountains, associated with health, happiness, love, and peace, provide a "home" for the protagonist. The plains, characterized by poor weather, suffering, disease, and death, are a place that is "not-home." Carlos Baker, who died in 1987, was the longtime chairman of the English Department at Princeton University. In addition to his highly acclaimed biography *Ernest Hemingway: A Life Story*, Baker wrote numerous novels, short stories, and poems.

The opening chapter of Hemingway's second novel, *A Farewell to Arms*, is a generically rendered landscape with thousands of moving figures. It does much more than start the book. It helps to establish the dominant mood (which is one of doom), plants a series of important images for future symbolic cultivation, and subtly compels the reader into the position of detached observer.

"In the late summer of that year we lived in a house in a village that looked across the river and the plain to the mountains. In the bed of the river there were pebbles and boulders, dry and white in the sun, and the water was clear and swiftly moving and blue in the channels. Troops went by the house and down the road and the dust they raised powdered the leaves of the trees. The trunks of the trees too were dusty and the leaves fell early that year and we saw the troops marching along the road and the dust rising and

Excerpted from Carlos Baker, *Hemingway: The Writer as Artist.* Copyright © 1956, 1963, 1972, renewed in 1980 by Princeton University Press. Reprinted with the permission of Princeton University Press. (Footnotes in the original have been omitted in this reprint.)

leaves, stirred by the breeze, falling and the soldiers marching and afterward the road bare and white, except for the leaves."

THE MOUNTAINS AND THE PLAIN

The first sentence here fixes the reader in a house in the village where he can take a long view across the river and the plain to the distant mountains. Although he does not realize it yet, the plain and the mountains (not to mention the river and the trees, the dust and the leaves) have a fundamental value as symbols. The autumnal tone of the language is important in establishing the autumnal mood of the chapter. The landscape itself has the further importance of serving as a general setting for the whole first part of the novel. Under these values, and of basic structural importance, are the elemental images which compose this remarkable introductory chapter.

The second sentence, which draws attention from the mountainous background to the bed of the river in the middle distance, produces a sense of clearness, dryness, whiteness, and sunniness which is to grow very subtly under the artist's hands until it merges with one of the novel's two dominant symbols, the mountain-image. The other major symbol is the plain. Throughout the substructure of the book it is opposed to the mountain-image. Down this plain the river flows. Across it, on the dusty road among the trees, pass the men-at-war, faceless and voiceless and unidentified against the background of the spreading plain.

In the third and fourth sentences of this beautifully managed paragraph the march-past of troops and vehicles begins. From the reader's elevated vantage-point, looking down on the plain, the river, and the road, the continuously parading men are reduced in size and scale—made to seem smaller, more pitiful, more pathetic, more like wraiths blown down the wind, than would be true if the reader were brought close enough to overhear their conversation or see them as individualized personalities.

Between the first and fourth sentences, moreover, Hemingway accomplishes the transition from late summer to autumn—an inexorability of seasonal change which prepares the way for the study in doom on which he is embarked. Here again the natural elements take on a symbolic function. In the late summer we have the dust; in the early autumn the dust and the leaves falling; and through them both the marching troops impersonally seen. The reminder, through the dust, of the words of the funeral service in the prayer-book is fortified by the second natural symbol, the falling leaves. They dry out, fall, decay, and become part of the dust. Into the dust is where the troops are going—some of them soon, all of them eventually.

RAIN AS SYMBOL

The short first chapter closes with winter, and the establishment of rain as a symbol of disaster. "At the start of the winter came the permanent rain and with the rain came the cholera. But it was checked and in the end only seven thousand died of it in the army." Already, now in the winter, seven thousand of the wraiths have vanished underground. The permanent rain lays the dust and rots the leaves as if they had never existed. There is no excellent beauty, even in the country around Gorizia, that has not some sadness to it. And there is hardly a natural beauty in the whole first chapter of *A Farewell to Arms* which has not some symbolic function in Hemingway's first study in doom. . . .

HOME AND NOT HOME

As its first chapter suggests, the natural-mythological structure which informs *A Farewell to Arms* is in some ways comparable to the Burguete-Montparnasse, Catholic-Pagan, and Romero-Cohn contrasts of *The Sun Also Rises*. One has the impression, however, of greater assurance, subtlety, and complexity in the second novel, as if the writing of the first had strengthened and consolidated Hemingway's powers and given him new insights into this method for controlling materials from below.

Despite the insistent, denotative matter-of-factness at the surface of the presentation, the subsurface activity of *A Farewell to Arms* is organized connotatively around two poles. By a process of accrual and coagulation, the images tend to build round the opposed concepts of Home and Not-Home. Neither, of course, is truly conceptualistic; each is a kind of poetic intuition, charged with emotional values and woven, like a cable, of many strands. The Home-concept, for example, is associated with the mountains; with dry-cold weather; with peace and quiet; with love, dignity, health, happiness, and the good life; and with worship or at least the consciousness of God. The Not-Home concept is associated with low-lying plains; with rain and fog; with obscenity, indignity, disease, suffering, nervousness, war and death; and with irreligion.

The motto of William Bird's Three Mountains Press in Paris, which printed Hemingway's *in our time*, was "Levavi oculos meos in montes [I lift up my eyes to the hills]." The line might also have served as an epigraph for *A Farewell to Arms*. Merely introduced in the first sentence of the first chapter, the mountain-image begins to develop important associations as early as Chapter Two. Learning that Frederick Henry is to go on leave, the young priest urges him to visit Capracotta in the Abruzzi. "There," he says, "is good hunting. You would like the people and though it is cold, it is clear and dry. You could stay with my family. My father is a famous hunter." But the lowlander infantry captain interrupts: "Come on," he says in pidgin Italian to Frederick Henry. "We go whorehouse before it shuts."

THE SYMBOLIC MOUNTAINS

After Henry's return from the leave, during which he has been almost everywhere else on the Italian peninsula *except* Abruzzi, the mountain-image gets further backing from another lowland contrast. "I had wanted," says he, "to go to Abruzzi. I had gone to no place where the roads were frozen and hard as iron, where it was clear cold and dry and the snow was dry and powdery and haretracks in the snow and the peasants took off their hats and called you Lord and there was good hunting. I had gone to no such place but to the smoke of cafés and nights when the room whirled and you needed to look at the wall to make it stop, nights in bed, drunk, when you knew that that was all there was."

Throughout Book I, Hemingway quietly consolidates the mountain-image. On the way up towards the Isonzo from Gorizia, Frederick looks across the river and the plain to the Julian and Carnic Alps. "I looked to the north at the two ranges of mountains, green and dark to the snow-line and then white and lovely in the sun. Then, as the road mounted along the ridge, I saw a third range of mountains, higher snow mountains, that looked chalky white and furrowed, with strange planes, and then there were mountains far beyond all these that you could hardly tell if you really saw.". . . Hemingway is using the mountains symbolically. Years later, in [his short story] "The Snows of Kilimanjaro," he would use the mighty peak of East Africa as a natural image of immortality, just as in *The Green Hills of Africa* he would build his narrative in part upon a contrast between the hill-country and the Serengeti Plain. When Frederick Henry lowers his eyes from the far off ranges, he sees the plain and the river, the war-making equipment, and "the broken houses of the little town" which is to be occupied, if anything is left of it to occupy, during the coming attack. Already now, a few dozen pages into the book, the mountain-image has developed associations; with the man of God and his homeland, with clear dry cold and snow, with polite and kindly people, with hospitality, and with natural beauty. Already it has its oppositions: the lowland obscenities of the priest-baiting captain, cheap cafés, one-night prostitutes, drunkenness, destruction, and the war.

When the trench-mortar explosion nearly kills Henry, the priest comes to visit him in the field-hospital, and the Abruzzi homeland acquires a religious association. "There in my country," says the priest, "it is understood that a man may love God. It is not a dirty joke." Repeating, for emphasis, the effect, of the priest's first account of the highland country, Hemingway allows Frederick to develop in his mind's eye an idyllic picture of the priest's home-ground.

"At Capracotta, he had told me, there were trout in the stream below the town. It was forbidden to play the flute at night . . . because it was bad for the girls to hear. . . . Aquila was a fine town. It was cool in the summer at night and the spring in Abruzzi was the most beautiful in Italy. But what was lovely was the fall to go hunting through the chestnut woods. The birds were all good because they fed on grapes, and you never took a lunch because the peasants were always honored if you would eat with them in their houses. . . ."

By the close of Book I, largely through the agency of the priest, a complex connection has come clear between the idea of Home and the combination of high ground, cold weather, love, and the love of God. Throughout, Hemingway has worked solely by suggestion, implication, and quiet repetition, putting the reader into potential awareness, readying him for what is to come.

CATHERINE BARKLEY

The next step is to bring Catherine Barkley by degrees into the center of the image. Her love affair with Henry begins as a "rotten game" of war-time seduction. Still emotionally unstable and at loose nervous ends from her fiancé's death, Catherine is a comparatively easy conquest. But in the American hospital at Milan, following Henry's ordeal by fire at the front not far from the Isonzo, the casual affair becomes an honorable though unpriested marriage. Because she can make a "home" of any room she occupies—and Henry several times alludes to this power of hers—Catherine naturally moves into association with ideas of home, love, and happiness. She does not really reach the center of the mountain-image until, on the heels of Frederick's harrowing lowland experiences during the retreat from Caporetto, the lovers move to Switzerland. Catherine is the first to go, and Henry follows her there as if she were the genius of the mountains, beckoning him on. Soon they are settled into a supremely happy life in the winterland on the mountainside above Montreux. Catherine's death occurs at Lausanne, after the March rains and the approaching need for a good lying-in hospital have driven the young couple down from their magic mountain—the closest approximation to the priest's fair homeland in the Abruzzi that they are ever to know.

The total structure of the novel is developed, in fact, around the series of contrasting situations already outlined. To Gorizia, the Not-Home of war, succeeds the Home which Catherine and Frederick make together in the Milan Hospital. The Not-Home of the grim retreat from the Isonzo is followed by the quiet and happy retreat which the lovers share above Montreux. Home ends for Frederick Henry when he leaves Catherine dead in the Lausanne Hospital.

Hemingway's Use of Details

Sheldon Norman Grebstein

Sheldon Norman Grebstein shows how minor details function to add depth and meaning to *A Farewell to Arms*. Grebstein analyzes the features of two passages, one early in the novel that depicts the objects in Frederic's room, another at the end in which a dog noses around in garbage cans. In each case, physical objects take on an emotional significance, as Hemingway translates details into drama. Sheldon Norman Grebstein has taught at the State University of New York at Binghamton. In addition to books on Hemingway, he has published works on Sinclair Lewis and John O'Hara.

In my discussion of individual works in previous chapters I have shown that the detailing of some little, seemingly insignificant gesture or movement—detail which in context melts into the overall verisimilitude [realistic nature] of the work... really performs the important function of cueing unstated emotion or attitude. This is a type of objective correlative [a phrase of the poet T.S. Eliot; used to suggest how objects can suggest emotions], or, to recall E.M. Halliday's apt phrase, objective epitome. However, even though the practice has already been noted, it is so pervasive in Hemingway's writing and yet so easy to overlook I want to return to the method and study it here at somewhat greater length. Two incidents in *A Farewell to Arms* will support what I have been saying about the tangibility of Hemingway's fictive world and demonstrate how detail manifests character and theme.

DETAILS OF FREDERIC'S ROOM

At the beginning of chapter 3 the protagonist returns from leave to his quarters near the front:

Excerpted from Sheldon Norman Grebstein, *Hemingway's Craft*. Copyright (1973) by Southern Illinois University Press. Reprinted by permission of the publisher.

> The room I shared with the lieutenant Rinaldi looked out on the courtyard. The window was open, my bed was made up with blankets and my things hung on the wall, the gas mask in an oblong tin can, the steel helmet on the same peg. At the foot of the bed was my flat trunk, and my winter boots, the leather shiny with oil, were on the trunk. My Austrian sniper's rifle with its blued octagon barrel and the lovely dark walnut, cheek-fitted, *schutzen* stock, hung over the two beds. The telescope that fitted it was, I remembered, locked in the trunk. The lieutenant, Rinaldi, lay asleep on the other bed. He woke when he heard me in the room and sat up.

Other than the necessary function of the passage to firmly reestablish Frederic in a military environment, why is such vivid and particular treatment given to the sniper's rifle, especially inasmuch as it is never mentioned again? Why the sharp focus on it, in a prose so carefully controlled and so wary of excess? The answer: because it tells something important about the protagonist.

Most obviously in the whole passage there is the pleasure in the order of things, the neat and precise disposition of objects in the immediate physical environment. We might call it Hemingway's pervasive desire for "a clean, well-lighted place" [the title of a famous Hemingway story]. This satisfies our predilection for order and helps us preserve the illusion of control over the threatening unruliness of the cosmos. So much we can share with Frederic Henry. But that military equipment, especially the deadly rifle, should be depicted in almost aesthetic terms ("lovely"), reveals an attribute, or attitude in Henry never spoken in the novel and, indeed, contrary to his mission in the ambulance unit as a saver of lives. What this episode really intimates is Frederic's boyish love of guns for their own sake and his lack of awareness of what guns do to human bodies. Consequently, Hemingway's momentary focus on the rifle returns us to the pre-Catherine, pre-separate peace, pre-reflective narrator condition of Frederic Henry, and suggests an unconfessed motivation for his military service at a time when his sensibility was on the same level as his gear: the boy's fascination with war, its adventure, and its accouterments.

Symbolic Details

Another little sequence of details, innocuous on the surface, appears soon after the opening of the novel's last chapter. Frederic has brought Catherine to the hospital and her labor has commenced. All proceeds normally and the mood is optimistic as Frederic goes out to get breakfast. On his way back to the hospital there is this seemingly lighthearted encounter:

> Outside along the street were the refuse cans from the houses waiting for the collector. A dog was nosing at one of the cans.
>
> "What do you want?" I asked and looked in the can to see if there was anything I could pull out for him; there was nothing on top but coffee-grounds, dust and some dead flowers.
>
> "There isn't anything, dog," I said.

But the true function of the passage belies its superficial cheerfulness. The mention of garbage cans and the scavenger dog strikes ominous warning notes: the cans and their contents are objective epitomes for the end of the tranquil domesticity the characters have briefly shared (coffee grounds), the demise of their love and of Catherine herself (dead flowers), and man's fate at large (dust). We might extend the symbolism just a little further and see the unsuccessfully searching dog as representative of Frederic himself, the narrator sifting through the debris of the past for something nourishing. Thus, the objective epitome does the work of a philosophical commentary on the vanity of human wishes—and also delineates the protagonist's altered condition—without the obtrusiveness and tedium of an actual commentary. By the use of objective detail, technique becomes a form of thought, translated into dramatic metaphor.

Hemingway's Baby Talk

Dwight Macdonald

In an essay on Hemingway from his book *Against the American Grain*, Dwight Macdonald parodies Hemingway's famous style in order to suggest the writer's weaknesses. When Hemingway was at his best, Macdonald asserts, his style was one of "inspired baby talk." At his worse he wrote "plain baby talk." Hemingway's simplicity of style is especially problematical in his novels, Macdonald maintains, where it becomes mannered and boring. He was far better as a writer of short stories. Even *A Farewell to Arms*, Hemingway's supposed best novel, contains numerous poorly written, redundant passages, MacDonald insists. Dwight Macdonald was a noted writer and editor for numerous magazines, including *Fortune, Partisan Review*, and the *New Yorker*. His books include the widely acclaimed *Parodies: An Anthology from Chaucer to Beerbohm—and After*.

He was a big man with a bushy beard and everybody knew him. The tourists knew him and the bartenders knew him and the critics knew him too. He enjoyed being recognized by the tourists and he liked the bartenders but he never liked the critics very much. He thought they had his number. Some of them did. The hell with them. He smiled a lot and it should have been a good smile, he was so big and bearded and famous, but it was not a good smile. It was a smile that was uneasy around the edges as if he was not sure he deserved to be quite as famous as he was famous.

INSPIRED BABY TALK

He liked being a celebrity and he liked celebrities. At first it was [American novelist] Sherwood Anderson and [American poet] Ezra Pound and [American writer] Gertrude Stein. He was an athletic young man from Oak Park, Illinois, who

Excerpted from Dwight Macdonald, *Against the American Grain* (New York: Random House, 1962), pp. 167–78. Copyright © 1952, 1953, 1954, © 1956, 1957, 1958, 1959, 1960, 1961, 1962 by Dwight Macdonald. Reprinted with the permission of the author's heirs. (Subheadings in this reprint have been added by the editor of the present volume.)

wanted to write and he made friends with them. He was always good at making friends with celebrities. They taught him about style. Especially Gertrude Stein. The short words, the declarative sentences, the repetition, the beautiful absence of subordinate clauses. He always worked close to the bull in his writing. In more senses than one *señor*. It was a kind of inspired baby talk when he was going good.* When he was not going good, it was just baby talk.** Or so the critics said and the hell with them. Most of the tricks were good tricks and they worked fine for a while especially in the short stories. Ernest was stylish in the hundred-yard dash but he didn't have the wind for the long stuff. Later on the tricks did not look so good. They were the same tricks but they were not fresh any more and nothing is worse than a trick that has gone stale. He knew this but he couldn't invent any new tricks. It was a great pity and one of the many things in life that you can't do anything about. Maybe that was why his smile was not a good smile.

The Tricks Stop Working

After 1930, he just didn't have it any more. His legs began to go and his syntax became boring and the critics began to ask why he didn't put in a few subordinate clauses just to make it look good. But the bartenders still liked him and the tourists liked him too. He got more and more famous and the big picture magazines photographed him shooting a lion and catching a tuna and interviewing a Spanish Republican militiaman and fraternizing with bullfighters and helping liberate Paris and always smiling bushily and his stuff got

---

*"And what if she should die? She won't die. People don't die in childbirth nowadays. That was what all husbands thought. Yes, but what if she should die? She won't die. She's just having a bad time. The initial labor is usually protracted. She's only having a bad time. Afterwards we'd say what a bad time, and Catherine would say it wasn't really so bad. But what if she should die? She can't die. Yes, but what if she should die? She can't, I tell you. Don't be a fool. It's just a bad time. It's just nature giving her hell. It's only the first labor, which is almost always protracted. Yes, but what if she should die? She can't die. Why should she die? What reason is there for her to die? . . . But what if she should die? She won't. She's all right. But what if she should die? She can't die. But what if she should die? Hey, what about that? What if she should die?"—*A Farewell to Arms*.

** I remember waking in the morning. Catherine was asleep and the sun was coming in through the window. The rain had stopped and I stepped out of bed and across the floor to the window. . . .
  "How are you, darling?" she said. "Isn't it a lovely day?"
  "How do you feel?"
  "I feel very well. We had a lovely night."
  "Do you want breakfast?"
  She wanted breakfast. So did I and we had it in bed, the November sunlight coming in through the window, and the breakfast tray across my lap.
  "Don't you want the paper? You always wanted the paper in the hospital."
  "No," I said. "I don't want the paper now."—*A Farewell to Arms*

worse and worse. Mr. Hemingway the writer was running out of gas but no one noticed it because Mr. Hemingway the celebrity was such good copy. It was all very American and in 1954 they gave him the Nobel Prize and it wasn't just American any more. The judges were impressed by "the style-forming mastery of the art of modern narration" he had shown in *The Old Man and the Sea*, which he had published in *Life* two years earlier. *Life* is the very biggest of the big picture magazines and *Life* is exactly where *The Old Man and the Sea* belonged. Literary-prize judges are not always clever. This is something you know and if you don't know it you should know it. They gave him the prize and the King of Sweden wrote to him. Mr. Hemingway meet Mr. Bernadotte.

After 1930 his friends were not named Anderson or Pound or Stein. They were named [hotel chain heir] Charles Ritz and [restauranteur] Toots Shor and [gossip columnist] Leonard Lyons and [Hollywood actors] Ava Gardner and Marlene Dietrich and Gary Cooper. He almost had a fight with Max Eastman because he thought Max Eastman had questioned his virility and he almost fought a duel with someone he thought might have insulted the honor of Ava Gardner but he didn't have the fight and he decided that Ava Gardner's honor had not been insulted after all. It is often difficult to tell about honor. It is something you feel in your *cojones*. Or somewhere. He liked Marlene Dietrich very much. They had good times together. He called her "The Kraut" and she called him "Papa." His wife called him "Papa" too. Many other people called him "Papa." He liked being called "Papa.". . .

A Farewell to Arms is generally considered Hemingway's best novel. It has aged and shriveled from what I remembered. I found myself skipping yards of this sort of thing:

"We could walk or take a tram," Catherine said.

"One will be along," I said. "They go by here."

"Here comes one," she said.

The driver stopped his horse and lowered the metal sign on his meter. The top of the carriage was up and there were drops of water on the driver's coat. His varnished hat was shining in the wet. We sat back in the seat and the top of the carriage made it dark.

[Half a page omitted]

At the hotel I asked Catherine to wait in the carriage while I went in and spoke to the manager. There were plenty of rooms. Then I went out to the carriage, paid the driver, and Catherine and I walked in together. The small boy in buttons carried the package. The manager bowed us towards the elevator. There was much red plush and brass. The manager went up in the elevator with us.

There is a great deal of paying cab drivers and finding it dark at night inside a closed carriage.

I found both the military part and the love story tedious except at moments of ordeal or catastrophe. The wounding of the narrator, Lieutenant Henry, and his escape after Caporetto are exciting, and the chapters on the retreat from Caporetto are as good as I remembered, especially the four pages about the shooting of the officers by the battle police. As long as the lieutenant and Catherine Barkley are making love and having "a good time" together, one is bored and skeptical. To my surprise, I found that Catherine was like the heroines of [Hemingway's later novels] *For Whom the Bell Tolls* and *Across the River and Into the Trees*, not a person but an adolescent daydream—utterly beautiful and utterly submissive and utterly in love with the dreamer: "You see I'm happy, darling, and we have a lovely time.... You are happy, aren't you? Is there anything I do you don't like? Can I do anything to please you? Would you like me to take down my hair? Do you want to play?" "Yes and come to bed." "All right. I'll go and see the patients first." The conversation of these lovers is even more protracted and boring than that of real lovers. (It is curious how verbose Hemingway's laconic style can become.) But at the end when Catherine dies in childbed, the feeling comes right and one is moved—just as the preceding ordeal of the escape to Switzerland by rowing all night is well done. This deathbed scene is one of the few successful ones in literary history; it is the stylistic antithesis to [British novelist Charles] Dickens' Death of Little Nell (of which [Irish writer]Oscar Wilde remarked, "One must have a heart of stone to read it without laughing").

HEMINGWAY WAS NOT A NOVELIST

The fact is Hemingway is a short-story writer and not a novelist. He has little understanding of the subject matter of the novel: character, social setting, politics, money matters, human relations, all the prose of life. Only the climactic moments interest him, and of those only ordeal, suffering, and death. (Except for a lyrical feeling about hunting and fishing.) In a novel he gets lost, wandering around aimlessly in a circle as lost people are said to do, and the alive parts are really short stories, such as the lynching of the fascists and the blowing up of the bridge in *For Whom the Bell Tolls*. In the short story he knows just where he is going and his style, which becomes tedious in a novel, achieves the intensity appropriate to the shorter form. The difference may be seen in comparing the dialogue in *A Farewell to Arms* with that in the little short story, "Hills like White Elephants," which is directed with superb craftsmanship to the single bitter point the story makes. Every line of this apparently random conversation between a man and a girl waiting at a Spanish railway station—she is going to Madrid for an abortion he wants but she doesn't—develops the theme and when toward the end she asks, "Would you do something for me now?" and he replies, "I'd do anything for you," and she says, "Would you please please please please please please please stop talking?"—then one feels that tightening of the scalp that tells one an artist has made his point.

A Simple Tale

Clifton Fadiman

For decades one of America's most influential critics, Clifton Fadiman considers the simplicity of A Farewell to Arms *to be among the novel's strongest features. This style goes against 1920s literary trends, when complex and difficult novels were the rule. But Hemingway's intensity of feeling comes through in his novel and ensures that he never excessively complicates his material. Two motifs, the love of woman and man and the friendship of comrades, drive the plot. Fadiman maintains that* A Farewell to Arms *is not a perfect novel, but it is a powerful and very American one. Clifton Fadiman has written and edited dozens of books, including* The Lifetime Reading Plan, The World Treasury of Children's Literature, *and* In Praise of E.B. White, Realist.

Recently [in the late 1920s] there have been laid down a number of dicta anent [rules about] what the modern novel may not do if it is to remain a modern novel. One of them is to the effect that a representation of a simple love affair is impossible in our day. Another tells us that it is difficult, if not impossible, to reproduce the emotion of male friendship or love, as the present shift in sex conventions tends to surround the theme with an ambiguous atmosphere. A third dictum concerns itself with the Impossibility of true tragedy in contemporary literature. A fourth, not so much a stated law as a pervasive feeling, would insist on the irrelevance to our time of the "non-intellectual" or "primitive" novel. Now, none of these generalizations is silly; there is a great deal of truth in all of them. It just happens that Mr. Hemingway, quite unconsciously, has produced a book which upsets all of them at once and so makes them seem more foolish than they really are. Worse still, his book is not merely a good book but a remarkably beautiful book; and it is not merely modern, but the very apotheosis of a kind of mod-

Reprinted from Clifton Fadiman, "A Fine American Novel," *The Nation*, October 30, 1929, by permission of *The Nation*.

ernism. Mr. Hemingway is simply one of those inconvenient novelists who won't take the trouble to learn the rules of the game. It is all very embarrassing.

A Simple Story

Take the business of love, for example. Neither Catherine nor Henry in "A Farewell to Arms" is a very complicated person. They are pretty intelligent about themselves but they are not over self-conscious. There are few kinks in their natures. I don't suppose they could produce one mental perversion between them. They fall in love in a simple, healthy manner, make love passionately and movingly; and when Catherine dies the reader is quite well aware that he has passed through a major tragic experience. Their story seems too simple to be "modern"; yet it is as contemporary as you wish. It seems too simple to be interesting; yet it is gripping, almost heartbreaking. I don't think any complex explanations are in order. I offer the familiar one that Hemingway, almost alone among his generation, feels his material very deeply and that he never overworks that material. Understatement is not so much a method with him as an instinctive habit of mind. (It is more or less an accident that it also happens to harmonize with the contemporary anti-romantic tendency.) Consequently we believe in his love story.

Similarly with the second motif of the book: the emotion of male affection, exemplified in the relationship between Henry and Rinaldi. This is the most perilous theme of all. With some of us a fake Freudism has inclined our minds to the cynical. Others, of simpler temperaments, inevitably think of comradeship in oozily sentimental terms, the [English writer Rudyard] Kipling strong-men-and-brothers-all business. Hemingway seems unaware of either attitude. Perhaps that unawareness partially explains his success. At any rate, without in any way straining our credulity he makes us feel that this very sense of comradeship—nordically reticent in Henry's case, blasphemously, ironically effusive in Rinaldi's—was one of the few things that mitigated the horror and stupidity of the war.

A Non-Intellectual Book

I have rarely read a more "non-intellectual" book than "A Farewell to Arms." This non-intellectuality is not connected with Hemingway's much discussed objectivity. It is implicit in his temperament. He is that marvelous combination—a highly intelligent naïf. I do not mean that he writes without thought, for as a matter of obvious fact he is one of the best craftsmen alive. But he feels his story entirely in emotional and narrative terms. He is almost directly opposed in temper, for example, to [American novelist] Sherwood Anderson, who would like to give the effect of naïvete but can't because he is always thinking about his own simplicity. "A Farewell to Arms" revolves about two strong, simple feelings: love for a beautiful and noble woman, affection for one's comrades. When it is not concerned with these two feelings it is simply exciting narrative—the retreat from Caporetto, the nocturnal escape to Switzerland. The whole book exists on a plane of strong feeling or of thrilling human adventure. It is impossible to feel superior to Hemingway's primitiveness, his insensibility to "ideas," because he strikes no attitude. A large part of the novel deals with simple things—eating cheese, drinking wine, sleeping with women. But he does not try to make you feel that these activities are "elemental" or overly significant. They are just integral parts of a personality which is strong and whole. Therein lies their effect on us. It is impossible to be patronizing about Henry's, or Hemingway's, complete contemporaneity, his mental divorcement from the past, the antique, the classical, the gentlemanly, cultured tradition. "The frescoes were not bad," remarks the hero at one point. "Any frescoes were good when they started to peel and flake off." This is not merely humorous; it is the reflection of a mind reacting freshly, freely, with an irony that is modern, yet simple and unaffected.

A GREAT AMERICAN NOVEL

"A Farewell to Arms" is not perfect by any means, nor, to me at least, interesting all the way through. I find the military descriptions dull, and for a paradoxical reason. Hemingway's crisp, curt, casual style, so admirably suited to the rest of his narrative, fails in the military portions because of these very qualities. It is too much like a regulation dispatch. Military reports have always been written in a sort of vulgar Hemingwayese; therefore they give no sense of novelty or surprise. But a detail like this does not matter much; the core of "A Farewell to Arms" remains untouched. It is certainly Hemingway's best book to date. There seems to be no reason why it should not secure the Pulitzer Prize for, despite the Italian setting, it is as American as Times Square. It is a real occasion for patriotic rejoicing.

Chronology

1899

Ernest Miller Hemingway born to Clarence and Grace Hemingway on July 21 in Oak Park, Illinois.

1914–1918

World War I; United States enters the war in 1917.

1917

Graduates from Oak Park High School; works as a cub reporter for the *Kansas City Star*.

1918

Works as an ambulance driver for the American Red Cross in World War I; wounded on July 8 on the Italian front; has an affair with nurse Agnes von Kurowsky, who later becomes the model for Catherine Barkley.

1919

The Treaty of Versailles formally ends World War I.

1920

Hemingway works as a reporter and foreign correspondent for the *Toronto Star*.

1921

Marries Hadley Richardson; moves to Paris on writer Sherwood Anderson's advice.

1922

Covers Greco-Turkish War for the *Toronto Star*.

1923

Three Stories and Ten Poems published by Robert McAlmon in Paris; birth of son John.

1924

In Our Time, a collection of vignettes, is published in Paris by Three Mountains Press.

1925

A second version of *In Our Time*, which adds fourteen short stories to the earlier vignettes, is published in New York by Boni and Liveright.

1926

The Torrents of Spring and *The Sun Also Rises* is published by Charles Scribner's Sons.

1927

Publishes short story collection, *Men Without Women*; divorces Richardson and marries Pauline Pfieffer.

1928

Moves to Key West, Florida; son Patrick is born; father commits suicide.

1929

A Farewell to Arms is published; the Great Depression begins.

1931

Son Gregory is born; Hemingway buys a home in Key West, and lives there for ten years.

1932

Death in the Afternoon is published.

1933

Publishes short story collection, *Winner Take Nothing*.

1935

Green Hills of Africa is published.

1936–1939

Spanish Civil War.

1937

Hemingway travels as a war correspondent to the Spanish Civil War; *To Have and Have Not* is published.

1938

Collaborates with Joris Ivens on *The Spanish Earth*, a film supporting the Loyalist cause; publishes *The Fifth Column* and *The First Forty-Nine Stories*.

1939–1945

World War II. The United States enters the war in 1941, after the Japanese bombing of Pearl Harbor.

1940

Hemingway divorces Pauline Pfieffer and marries Martha Gellhorn; purchases Finca Vigia in Cuba; *For Whom the Bell Tolls* is published.

1942–1945

Covers World War II in Europe as a newspaper and magazine correspondent; also covers the war in China.

1942

Edits *Men at War.*

1944

Meets Mary Welsh in London; covers the Allied liberation of Paris.

1945

Divorces Martha Gellhorn.

1946

Marries Mary Welsh.

1950

Across the River and into the Trees is published.

1951

Grace Hall Hemingway, the writer's mother, dies.

1952

The Old Man and the Sea is published.

1953

Receives Pulitzer Prize for *The Old Man and the Sea.*

1954

Receives Nobel Prize in literature.

1960

Moves to Ketchum, Idaho; hospitalized for uncontrolled high blood pressure, liver disease, diabetes, depression.

1961

Commits suicide in Ketchum, Idaho, on July 2.

FOR FURTHER RESEARCH

ABOUT ERNEST HEMINGWAY

Carlos Baker, *Hemingway: A Life Story*. New York: Scribner's, 1961.

Sheridan Baker, *Ernest Hemingway: An Introduction and Interpretation*. New York: Holt, Rinehart & Winston, 1967.

Denis Brian, *The True Gen: An Intimate Portrait of Hemingway by Those Who Knew Him*. New York: Grove, 1988.

Anthony Burgess, *Ernest Hemingway and His World*. New York: Scribner's, 1978.

Peter Griffin, *Along with Youth: Hemingway, The Early Years*. New York: Oxford University Press, 1985.

Leicester Hemingway, *My Brother, Ernest Hemingway*. Cleveland, OH: World, 1961.

A.E. Hotchner, *Papa Hemingway: A Personal Memoir*. New York: Random House, 1966.

Richard B. Hovey, *Hemingway: The Inward Terrain*. Seattle: University of Washington Press, 1968.

Kenneth S. Lynn, *Hemingway*. New York: Simon and Schuster, 1987.

James R. Mellow, *Hemingway: A Life Without Consequences*. Boston: Houghton Mifflin, 1992.

Jeffrey Meyers, *Hemingway: A Biography*. New York: Harper & Row, 1985.

Michael Reynolds, *Hemingway: The American Homecoming*. Malden, MA: Blackwell, 1992.

———, *Hemingway: The Paris Years*. Malden, MA: Blackwell, 1989.

———, *The Young Hemingway*. Malden, MA: Blackwell, 1986.

Earl Rovit, *Ernest Hemingway*. New York: Twayne, 1963.

Henry S. Villard and James Nagel, *Hemingway in Love and War: The Lost Diary of Agnes von Kurowsky*. Boston: Northeastern University Press, 1989.

About *A Farewell to Arms*

Carlos Baker, ed., *Ernest Hemingway: Critiques of the Four Major Novels.* New York: Scribner's, 1962.

Scott Donaldson, ed., *New Essays on* A Farewell to Arms. Cambridge, England: Cambridge University Press, 1990.

Leslie Fiedler, *Love and Death in the American Novel.* New York: Stein and Day, 1975.

Jay Gellens, ed., *Twentieth-Century Interpretations of* A Farewell to Arms. Englewood Cliffs, NJ: Prentice-Hall, 1970.

Nicholas J. Karolide, Lee Burress, and John M. Kean, eds., *Censored Books: Critical Viewpoints.* Metuchen, NJ: Scarecrow Press, 1993.

Katie de Koster, ed., *Ernest Hemingway.* Literary Companion series. San Diego: Greenhaven, 1997.

Bernard Oldsey, *Hemingway's Hidden Craft: The Writing of* A Farewell to Arms. University Park: Pennsylvania State University Press, 1979.

Robert Penn Warren, Introduction to *A Farewell to Arms.* New York: Scribner's, 1957.

About World War I

Vera Brittain, *Testament of Youth.* New York, Macmillan, 1935.

George H. Cassar, *The Forgotten Front: The British Campaign in Italy 1917–1918.* London: Hambledon, 1998.

John Ellis, *Eye-Deep in Hell : Trench Warfare in World War I.* Baltimore: Johns Hopkins University Press, 1989.

Robert Graves, *Goodbye to All That.* Garden City, NY: Doubleday, 1959.

Siegfried Sassoon, *The Complete Memoirs of George Sherston.* London: Faber and Faber, 1972.

James L. Stokesbury, *A Short History of World War I.* New York: William Morrow, 1981.

Peter Vansittart, *Voices from the Great War.* New York: Avon, 1985.

J.W. Wilks and E.M. Wilks, "The British Army in Italy 1917–1918," *Pen & Sword,* July 1998.

J.M. Winter, *The Experience of World War I.* New York: Oxford University Press, 1989.

Index

Across the River and into the Trees (Hemingway), 27–28, 88, 145
Against the American Grain (Macdonald), 142
Á la recherché du temp perdu (Proust), 121–22
Aldington, Richard, 41, 123
Aldridge, John W., 110
"All Armies Are the Same" (Hemingway), 85
All Quiet on the Western Front (Remarque), 41
Anderson, Sherwood, 21, 149

Baker, Carlos, 16, 20, 53, 54, 124, 133
Beach, Joseph Warren, 100
Beach, Sylvia, 19
Bell, Millicent, 50, 52–53
Bennett, Arnold, 24
Benson, Jackson J., 50, 55, 83
"Big Two-Hearted River" (Hemingway), 21
Braque, Georges, 19
Brave New World (Orwell), 86
Bridges, Robert, 46
Brumback, Ted, 14–15, 19

Cabot, John, 28
Canby, Henry Seidel, 24
Castle, The (Kafka), 86
Castro, Fidel, 29
Catcher in the Rye (Salinger), 67
characters

Bonello, 108, 109
Catherine Barkley, 30, 58, 148
  commitment to Frederic, 52–53
  critics' response to, 49–50
  deathbed scene of, 145
  drive to obliterate herself, 61
  as hero, 50, 55, 73
  and home concept, 138
  neuroses of, 51–52
  reversal of roles with Frederic, 53–54, 75–76
Count Greffi, 31, 35, 98
  view of love, 60, 103
Ettore Moretti, 31, 107
  satirical treatment of, 90
Frederic Henry, 11, 18, 30, 148
  as anti-hero, 73–74
  child-like depiction of, 52–53, 57–50, 140
  complicity of, in corruption of war, 57
  education of, 69–71
  on embarrassment by abstractions, 41
  existential awakening of, 99
  general unawareness of, 84
  interior monologue of, on Catherine's death, 73
  banalities of, 79
  love for Catherine is exploitative, 62–66
  as narrator
    change in viewpoint of, 125–26

opinions of, are not trustworthy, 67
retrospective view of, 72
position of, between priest and Rinaldi, 102
realization of war as irrational, 92–94
rejection of generalities by, 80
reversal of roles with Catherine, 53–54
magnifies his negative identity, 75
river escape of, 110
shooting of deserters by, 108
stages of relationship with Catherine, 131
view of war vs. defeat, 87–88
wounding of, and loss of immortality, 88–89
Gino, 107
Helen Ferguson, 31, 53, 59
Passini, 87–88, 91
irony in death of, 89
the priest, 58
description of love, 51, 60
idealism in, 111
as Frederic's mentor, 69, 70
and symbolism of mountains, 136, 137
view of war, 101
Rinaldi, 30, 58, 148
cynicism and devoutness of, 91
model for, 17
transformation of, 69–70, 92
view of war, 101–102
cliché
Frederic's use of, 79–80
and final rejection of, 81–82
Cowley, Malcolm, 24, 42
on baptism of Frederic, 109–10
Crane, Stephen, 39
Criterion, The (magazine), 42
cummings, e.e., 10

Dangerous Summer, The (Hemingway), 29

Death in the Afternoon (Hemingway), 25, 132
Death of a Hero (Aldington), 41, 123
details
in description of Frederic's room, 139–40
Dickens, Charles, 145
Didion, Joan, 120
Donaldson, Scott, 53, 55, 56
Dos Passos, John, 15, 22, 29

Eliot, George, 116
Eliot, T.S., 42, 123, 139

Fadiman, Clifton, 24. 147
Farewell to Arms, A, 10
conflicts in, 106
critical response to, 41–42, 116
defies rules about modern novel, 147–48
earlier beginning of, 117–18
earlier ending of, 40
film version of, 25, 42–43
as modern morality drama, 84
plot of, 31–36
revision of, 23–24
as romantic novel, 132
selection of title for, 55, 126, 129
values embodied in, 105
Faulkner, William, 11
Fetterley, Judith, 49
Fiedler, Leslie, 49
Fisher, Deborah, 50
Fitzgerald, F. Scott, 20, 29, 116, 119, 122
Flaubert, Gustave, 55, 122
Ford, Ford Madox, 21, 121
For Whom the Bell Tolls (Hemingway), 10, 26, 145, 146
Fussell, Paul, 44

Galantiere, Lewis, 19
Gelfant, Blanche, 78
Gellhorn, Martha "Marty" (third wife), 26
Goodbye to All That (Graves), 41

Graves, Robert, 41
Grebstein, Sheldon Norman, 51, 139
Green Hills of Africa, The, (Hemingway), 25, 137
Gurko, Leo, 73

Hackett, Francis, 108
Haggard, Rider, 46
Halliday, E.M., 67, 139
Hays, Peter L., 49
Hemingway, Clarence Edmonds (father), 13, 18
  suicide of, 23
Hemingway, Ernest
  as ambulance driver, 15–16
  birth of, 12
  childhood of, 13–14
  composition sense of, 125–26
  defied rules for modern novel, 147–48
  on events surrounding the writing of novel, 38
  in Key West, 25
  as model for his protagonists, 12, 25
  in Paris, 19–20
  as reporter for *Kansas City Star,* 14–15
  return to Oak Park, 17–19
  in Spanish Civil War, 26
  suicide of, 29
  theory of inventing from knowledge, 38–40
  view of love given by, 104
  on vocabulary of war, 10–11
  war efforts of, 26–27
  wins Nobel Prize, 28
  on wounding at Italian front, 16
Hemingway, Grace Hall (mother), 12–13, 16, 18, 19, 25
Hemingway, John Hadley Nicanor (son), 20
Hemingway, Patrick (son), 22
Henty, George Alfred, 46
heroes

Catherine Barkley as, 50, 55, 73, 130
  in Hemingway
    represents many men, 128
    test of Frederic as, 79
"Hills like White Elephants" (Hemingway), 146
Hindmarsh, Harry, 21
Hotchner, A.E., 29

imagery
  use in place of argument/exposition, 85
"In Another Country" (Hemingway), 122
"Indian Camp" (Hemingway), 21, 23
In Our Time (Hemingway), 18, 21, 85, 122, 127
irony, 90–91
  of death in unexpected forms, 124–25
  in Frederic's normality, 83–84
  in Frederic's view of war, 85
  of World War I, 44

Jessup, Elsie, 54
Jimmy Breen (Hemingway), 22

Kafka, Franz, 86
Kansas City Star, 14
Kert, Bernice, 54
Kesey, Ken, 52
Kipling, Rudyard, 148

La Farge, Oliver, 11
Larkin, Philip, 44
Laughing Boy (La Farge), 11
Lewis, Robert, 53
Lewis, Sinclair, 39
Loeb, Harold, 20, 40
"lost generation," 100
Lynn, Kenneth, 12, 16, 24

Macdonald, Dwight, 142
Martin, Wendy, 49
Marvell, Andrew, 98
Matisse, Henri, 19

McAlmon, Robert, 20
"MCMXIV" (Larkin), 44
Mellow, James R., 12, 16
Men at War (Hemingway, ed.), 27
metaphor
  war as, for mass man, 86–87
Meyers, Jeffrey, 17, 38
Miller, D. Quentin, 85
Morris, William, 46
mortality
  awareness of, and time, 98–99
  Frederic's wounding and realization of, 88–89
  Great War elicited confrontation with, 95
  objective epitomes for, 141
Moveable Feast, A (Hemingway), 29

objective correlative, 123
  definition of, 123
Old Man and the Sea, The (Hemingway), 10, 28, 144
Oldsey, Bernard, 55, 116
One Flew Over the Cuckoo's Nest (Kesey), 52
O'Neill, Eugene, 51
Orwell, George, 86
Owen, Wilfred, 10

Parker, Dorothy, 24
pathetic fallacy, 130–31
Peele, George, 127, 129
Perkins, Maxwell, 20, 22, 23, 119
  on choice of title, 126
  death of, 27
Pfeiffer, Gus, 41
Pfeiffer, Pauline (second wife), 22
Picasso, Pablo, 19
plot, 31–36
  cliché as device of, 82
poém en prose (prose-poem), 122–23
  in chapter I, 123
  as foreshadow, 124
Pound, Ezra, 19, 20, 29

Priestley, J.B., 42
Proust, Marcel, 121–22
Pulitzer Prize, 10–11

Remarque, Erich, 41
Reynolds, Michael S., 50, 53, 55, 72
Richardson, Hadley (first wife), 19, 21
Rovit, Earl, 55

Salinger, J.D., 67
Sassoon, Siegfried, 10
Serena, Enrico, 17
"Short Happy Life of Francis Macomber, The" (Hemingway), 25
"Snows of Kilimanjaro, The" (Hemingway), 25, 122, 136
"Soldier's Home" (Hemingway), 18
Sound and the Fury, The (Faulkner), 11
Stallings, Laurence, 42
Stein, Gertrude, 19, 20, 21, 29, 100, 143
Strange Interlude (O'Neill), 51
Stuckey, W.J., 11
style, 130
  Hemingway's
    in short story vs. novel, 145–46
  Stein's influence on, 143
  rejection of generalities in, 114
Sun Also Rises, The (Hemingway), 10, 57, 100, 119, 127
  characters
    inspiration for, 21
    Jake Barnes, 105, 128
  publication of, 22
symbols
  ants on log, of determinist universe, 66–67
  battle police at bridge as
    of abstraction and generality, 109
    of non-meaning, 92

mountains and plains, 134, 136
rain, 135
for disaster, 130-31
scavenging dog, 66-67, 141
seasonal change, 134-35
water images, 124

Taylor, A.J.P., 45
Tender Is the Night, 119
Tennyson, Alfred, Lord, 46
themes
  home vs. not-home concept, 135-36
  love, 83, 110-11
    definitions of, 50-51, 102-103
    Hemingway's understated treatment of, 148
    as refuge from failures of generalities, 112
    sacred vs. profane, contrast between, 59-60
  male affection, 148
  marriage
    as a convention, 111-12
    sanctity of, 103
  religion, 113
  stoic response to malign universe, 41
  and style, rejection of generalities in, 114
  war, 83, 106-107
    destruction of idealism by, 41
Three Stories and Ten Poems, 20
time
  Frederic's fear of, 96-98
  references to
    lack of, in early chapters, 95-96
    in later chapters, 99
Times, 46
Tolstoy, Leo, 39
Toronto Star Weekly, 18, 20
Torrents of Spring, The

(Hemingway), 21
Transatlantic Review, 21
Trapeze (school newspaper), 14
Twysden, Lady Duff, 21

U.S.A. (Dos Passos), 15

"Very Short Story, A" (Hemingway), 127
von Kurowsky, Agnes, 17, 18, 22, 52

Waldhorn, Arthur, 68
Walsh, Mary (fourth wife), 27
war
  destruction of idealism by, 41
  endlessness of, and concept of time, 95-96
  euphemistic language of, 46-47
  Frederic's ironic view of, 85
  literary treatment of, 10-11
  and loss of self, 86-87
War and Peace (Tolstoy), 39
Warren, Robert Penn, 110, 112
Watkins, Floyd C., 106
Wellington, C.G. "Pete," 14
Wexler, Joyce, 50, 51
Whitehead, Alfred North, 114
Whitlow, Roger, 50
Whitman, Walt, 10
Wilde, Oscar, 145
Wilson, Edmund, 121
Wolfe, Thomas, 119
women
  Hemingway's portrayal of, 49, 145
World War I
  loss of innocence following, 44-46
  portrayal of, by modern writers, 10-11
Wylder, Delbert, 50

Young, Philip, 29, 49, 127